B&T
$4.75
21 Feb '78

THE BOBBS-MERRILL STUDIES IN SOCIOLOGY

# Man And Earth: Their Changing Relationship

Gail W. Finsterbusch

THE BOBBS-MERRILL COMPANY, INC.
INDIANAPOLIS

Copyright © 1977 by The Bobbs-Merrill Company, Inc.

Printed in the United States of America

All rights reserved. No part of this book shall be reproduced or transmitted in any form or by any means, electronic or mechanical, including photocopying, recording, or by any information or retrieval system, without written permission from the Publisher:

> The Bobbs-Merrill Company, Inc.
> 4300 West 62nd Street
> Indianapolis, Indiana 46268

First Edition
First Printing 1977

**Library of Congress Cataloging in Publication Data**
Finsterbusch, Gail W
  Man and earth, their changing relationship.

  (The Bobbs-Merrill studies in sociology)
  Bibliography: p.
  1. Human ecology. 2. Anthropo-geography.
I. Title.
GF41.F56         301.31         76-26914

ISBN 0-672-61325-5

# Man And Earth:
# Their Changing Relationship

1 **Introduction**
2 **The Agricultural Era**
   Irrigation
   The Harnessing of Energy
   Old and New World Crop
      and Livestock Exchange
   Agrichemicals
   Selective Breeding and Genetics
3 **The Industrial Era**
   Rapid Technological Advance
   Population Explosion and Urbanization
   The Pursuit of Material Abundance
4 **A New Era of Accommodation**
   Resource Constraints
   Ecological Stresses
   Changing Attitudes and Behavior Toward Population Growth
   Moderating High Consumption
   Toward a More Perspicacious Technology
   Distribution—the New Insistent Issue
5 **Lifeboat Ethics?**

**References**

# 1 Introduction

The earth is changing. It has always changed. A sedimentary record spanning much of the earth's 4.6 billion year history attests to the continuance of change throughout past ages. Species have come and gone; many more have gone than have remained. Climates have shifted, mountains have risen and worn away, continents have split and moved thousands of miles to open new seas. On this geological time scale the history of man is astonishingly small. According to recent human fossil bone finds in Ethiopia, man appeared in the earth's biosphere at least 4 million years ago. Yet, this appearance is still very recent, a mere 3.1 seconds ago, if one imagines the earth to be an hour old. The first great ice age in the fossil record occurred 250 to 300 million years ago and lasted 30 to 50 million years. The most recent great ice age started some 5 million years ago in the southern hemisphere, and about 2.5 million years ago in the north. A retreat of ice that began eight to sixteen thousand years ago has left the world we know now.

Modern man, one species among the millions, has acquired the power to affect the whole earth in many ways. Knowingly or unknowingly, he has introduced or accelerated changes in the earth's chemistry, its *biota* or living systems, and now its climate. This new challenge for man—the twentieth-century challenge of the environment—will grow more and more acute. Only now is man recognizing that this is a new and unique situation, an unfamiliar era of promise and danger which lies beyond human experience. Even the rich technological and industrial societies require some extraordinary innovations in science and technology, and in the values, behavior, and efforts of individuals everywhere. There are no purely "technical solutions." However, there is widespread agreement that human welfare hinges on the basic integrity of the earth's biosphere.

Throughout most of man's existence the supply of food has sharply limited his numbers and lifestyle. He lived for hundreds of millennia, more than 99 percent of his existence, as a predator, a scavenger, and a primitive food collector. Preagricultural man, like the lion and other predators, remained by force of the conditions of his existence relatively scarce and sparse in the uncontrolled balance of nature. While living on wild food during the first 4 million years, his numbers never exceeded 10 million, a planetary population smaller than that of London, Ohio, or Nepal today. Before agriculture, man spread around the world to all continents except Antarctica, surviving on whatever wild food could be found, living in small groups for the most part, and wandering over considerable distances, migrating with the prey and with the seasons. Man competed with other species for the same food supply—as is still the case in the competition between bushmen and cheetahs in Africa today. And he was, himself, consumed as food by other predators, including humans. During this long hunting era, almost the whole of life was spent on the move, living in this or that cave, or perhaps in a few half-buried shelters. Human groups, like those of other species, often staked out territory and held it in common, but because life was mainly a search for food, there were no permanent villages or campsites. Living conditions were universally meager and starvation was a constant threat. There was no woven cloth, no pottery, no utensils, and no time during a lifespan for much of anything except protection and the quest for food. Very few were freed from hunting and gathering, with men as the hunters primarily, and women as the gatherers. Probably more than half the humans who have ever lived on earth lived prior to agriculture.

Man is an omnivore. He is able to eat, and does eat, almost anything edible that grows on the planet, even the most poisonous plants and animals once the poison has been removed. Australian aborigines, for example, think nothing of catching a poisonous snake, biting off its head, skinning it, and then eating it. For millennia man has prepared and eaten as a dietary staple the bitter *manioc* plant, which is toxic in the raw state. This omnivorous nature has enabled him to inhabit all the diverse environments of the globe where plant and animal life were plentiful enough to keep him alive. Human hunting groups were also able to endure the rhythm of feast and famine, eating prodigiously whenever food was abundant, surviving on short supplies when necessary, and going completely without food for considerable periods.

As a hunter, man had become the most inventive and adaptive of animals. He created a spoken language, early art, and notation systems. He had developed refined hunting tools and ingenious techniques, plus had the use of fire for perhaps a million years—although not universally. In some parts of the world, he changed considerably the prevailing natural ecosystem. The complex plant and animal life, now characteristic of the grassy plains in East Africa, for example, dates back some two hundred thousand years. It is now thought to be the result of man's successive burning of early forests to hunt animals, and to look out over expanses of flat land. In the new world, there is evidence that overhunting by big game hunters, organized on an extensive and efficient scale, may have caused the extinction of large mammal species during a short 300 year period, ten to twelve thousand years ago. But whatever capacity man the hunter had for intervening in the environment and altering the earth, was exceedingly limited compared with what was to come for man after the invention of agriculture.

# 2 The Agricultural Era

The great transition from hunter to tiller began perhaps as recently as twelve to fifteen thousand years ago when humans discovered how to domesticate plants and animals. The invention of agriculture changed man's relation to the environment radically, enabling him to move beyond the limits on his numbers and density, and on his lifestyle, social organization, and values set by unmanaged nature. He could now shape the environment to suit his needs. This profound change which freed him from the hunt, gave him new perceptions and expectations of nature. It brought new obligations as well, increasingly tying him to the land. (See Dalrymple, 1974; McNeill, 1965; and Sagan, 1975.)

At first only a handful were attracted to the new, more settled way of life. But over the millennia it became the preferred way. Today only a small fraction of the human race lives by hunting. Man substituted the vagaries of weather for the uncertainty of the hunt.

The origins of agriculture are still a mystery, but some of the earliest evidence of the revolutionary change in man's role from hunter and food gatherer, to herdsman and tiller is found in western Asia in the uplands bordering the Tigris-Euphrates valley. Climate was hospitable there, providing generous winter and spring rainfall to revive grasses that had withered during the summer drought. Food resources such as wheat, barley, peas, and lentils grew wild there and were relatively abundant, as were the sheep, goats, pigs, cattle, asses, deer, gazelles, horses, and dogs.

Sometime after 10000 B.C., groups of hunters and gatherers living in the hills around the fertile crescent began to move out of their caves into semipermanent encampments and, in some places, to more permanent sites or hunting villages. People living in most of these camps and settlements still hunted or collected most of their food. But available evidence indicates that man was intensively collecting food, and was perhaps experimenting with domestication. Certainly, although incidentally, he was accumulating experience and familiarity with the species that were eventually domesticated. The discoverers and inventors were people making the transition from cave dweller to villager, hinting at a change in awareness and a conscious effort to produce food.

Both animal and plant domestication appear to extend back to at least 9000 B.C. in southwestern Asia. Remains there suggest that animals were domesticated before plants and that sheep were the earliest animal domesticates. Wheat and barley were probably the first plants domesticated, although peas and lentils were also cultivated at an early date. In hunting societies everywhere, women were more than likely the inventors of plant-food cultivation. They had greater familiarity with plants and had better opportunities for observing, for example, the relation between seeds accidentally dropped and subsequent germination.

Knowledge of farming spread throughout the world. It moved eastward across Asia, southward into the Tigris-Euphrates region, and then along the Nile into Africa, and northwestward into Europe through the Danube valley and along the Mediterranean coast. By at least 6000 B.C. agricultural villages appear to have stretched across a 2,500-mile zone from Afghanistan in the east, to Greece in the west. Before 5000 B.C. the agrarian way of life was moving down into the alluvial river plains of the Tigris-Euphrates valley. By around 3000 B.C. all the plains in western Eurasia lying south of the Scandinavian mountains were inhabited by settlers living in more or less permanent villages. They cultivated a variety of crops, raised goats, sheep, cattle, and pigs, and cut the deciduous forest with stone axes.

Agriculture apparently had independent origins in the Americas, southeastern Asia, and perhaps China with centers of origin in the Americas being the Andean highlands, the Amazon basin, and Middle America. This opinion is not held universally, for some feel that the idea of agriculture spread over land and sea, reaching the Americas either through migration over the Bering Strait or voyages across the Pacific. But it is certain that nine thousand years ago beans and squash were being cultivated in the New World. In Thailand evidence is accumulating that man was cultivating rice twelve to fifteen thousand years ago, even earlier than in western Asia. Whether agriculture in China began independently or by diffusion from both southwestern and monsoon Asia is still an open question. Many scholars think that the agricultural techniques and domesticated species from both places met and mingled in northern China in the Yellow River valley sometime in the third millennium B.C.

Over a period of time man cleared billions of acres of forests and grasslands and planted crops that better suited his needs. Grassland on which wild animals grazed was eventually planted with grasses that had larger, more easily consumable seeds, such as wheat, barley, rye, oats, rice and millets. Wheat alone covers some 600 million acres, an area equivalent to the United States east of the Mississippi, that once supported wild grasses, forests, and the associated wild animals. Today crops cover some 3.6 billion acres—about 11 percent of the earth's total land surface and a considerably larger fraction of the area capable of supporting vegetation. Two-thirds of the planet's cropland is planted to cereal.

Livestock have tended to increase in number commensurately with human population. Today the global farmyard consists of more than 3.5 billion animals, almost one-third of which are cattle. Cows, first domesticated in southwest Asia, spread with man to the four corners of the earth. They displaced the massive herds of bison (once numbering an estimated 30 to 40 million) in North America; replaced the reindeer in Europe; took over the kangaroo territory in Australia; and now compete with the zebra, gazelle and other hoofed animals for grass on the East African plateau. They thrive on the Argentine Pampas and fill the great river valleys of Asia.

The earliest domesticated plants and animals continue to dominate the human food supply. Domesticated at the beginning in Old and New World centers of origin, wheat, barley, rice, corn and potatoes fill contemporary farm fields and still remain man's staple crops. With the exception of tomatoes and coffee, man has not domesticated any important new food plants in the last two thousand years. He lives on relatively few of the five-hundred thousand to one million plant species on earth. Similarly, the first animals to be domesticated for the purpose of food (sheep, goats, cattle, and pigs) remain man's major food animals. In ancient Egypt, attempts to domesticate deer and gazelles were unsuccessful, as were nineteenth-century attempts with zebras. The great shift in importance from animal to vegetable food sources is probably the most significant change in mankind's diet since the start of the agricultural era. The human diet today is dominated by cereals, which provide more than half of the food energy intake. Globally, only 12 percent of the human food energy supply measured in calories comes from livestock products and fish. This proportion is much higher in some parts of the world—North America's intake is around 31 percent, Western Europe about 22 percent, Oceania 36 percent; in Asia, it is less than 5 percent. Only Canada, the United States, Australia, and New Zealand derive more calories from livestock than from starchy foods.

Following domestication, the history of agriculture is punctuated with five predominant technological advances that enlarged man's capacity to intervene in natural systems. The discovery of irrigation; the harnessing of power both draft and mechanical for agricultural purposes; the exchange of crops between Old and New Worlds; the knowledge and use of agricultural chemicals, particularly fertilizers; and advances in genetics, particularly plant genetics, further expanded the earth's food-producing capacity.

# IRRIGATION

After the invention of agriculture, irrigation was man's next major effort to alter the natural functioning of the earth's ecosystem in the quest for more food. Irrigation is simply an intervention by humans in the sun-powered natural cycling of water. Farmers discovered early that they could augment limited rainfall by obstructing the flow of water in rivers and streams and diverting it into their fields through ditches and canals. A distinctly irrigated agriculture emerged as early as six thousand years ago in the Tigris-Euphrates valley and along the Nile as well. Soil in these valleys was light and very fertile, but in need of water. Irrigated agriculture provided the surplus food and spurred the social organization associated with the rise of the earliest river valley civilizations.

Nature distributes rainfall very unevenly over the earth. Modification of the hydrologic cycle enabled humans to bring vast areas of the world that would otherwise be unusable or only marginally productive into profitable cultivation. Irrigation has also been used to intensify agriculture by raising yields on land already cultivated. All modern irrigation systems, such as those in Japan or in California, will deliver five times as much water to a given land area as traditional systems, which were essentially defensive, designed mainly to protect crops against drought. Increasing control of water in countries such as Japan and Israel has been a dominant feature of the intensification of agriculture.

In 1800 an estimated 20 million acres of the world's cropland were irrigated, and by 1900 the figure had reached 100 million. A virtual explosion in irrigated acreage has occurred in the twentieth century, with a fivefold increase to around 500 million acres in 1975. Most of the irrigated acreage is in Asia, devoted to rice cultivation. The tremendous demand for food during the current century in which human population moved from 1.4 to 4 billion, has been the major impetus for growth in irrigated land.

Rivers have always been the major source of irrigation water. In the twentieth century, the intervention into the hydrologic cycle has extended to more and more rivers and to larger and more tightly managed irrigation systems (see Dalrymple, 1974; McNeill, 1965; Sagan, 1975; and Ehrlich et al., 1976). Fertile but dry agricultural land is available in many areas of the earth if water can be found to make it productive. Yet today, most of the rivers that easily lend themselves to damming and irrigation have already been developed. The remaining rivers to be exploited for irrigation are the Mekong, the Congo, and the Amazon, but these are very difficult to harness. With easy opportunities to construct new irrigation reservoirs diminishing, the expansion of the world's irrigated acreage will tend to recede. In the future, efforts to expand water supplies for agriculture must increasingly center on more massive and complex interventions into the hydrologic cycle, using such techniques as the diversion and redirecting of rivers, the manipulation of rainfall and snowfall patterns and, depending on energy costs, the desalting of seawater. One such development scheme suggests linking all the rivers on the Indo-Pakistan subcontinent into one system for irrigation, transport, and power.

Even in antiquity some of man's technological intrusions in the hydrologic cycle exceeded his understanding of them, particularly of the subterranean dynamics of rising water tables resulting in waterlogging and salting of soil. Remains of civilizations buried beneath desert sands in Mesopotamia and elsewhere in the Middle East and even in parts of the New World attest to man's incomplete knowledge of the consequences. Flying over Iraq and West Pakistan, it is possible to see miles and miles of salt-whitened land on which crops once grew and man-the-tiller flourished. Fortunately, new small-scale irrigation systems consisting of tubewells and pumps are helping to reclaim salted land in Pakistan by drawing groundwater up, and thereby lowering the water table and washing toxic salts downward. Large-scale systems such as the Aswan in Egypt, the Volta River Project in Ghana, the Colorado River System in the United States, and some of the more massive irrigation systems in Asia are displacing human populations and altering the environment profoundly. Because it illustrates graphically the interaction between man's hopes and efforts to expand his prosperity and his ignorance of the full consequences of his interventions, it is worth dwelling briefly on Egypt's Aswan system. When the first Aswan dam was completed in 1902, there was no comparable structure anywhere in the world. With year-round irrigation possible on large acreages, agriculture prospered, population grew, and the thirst for water mounted. The Aswan system was enlarged several times, culminating in the Aswan High Dam, inaugurated in 1971 (Sterling, 1971).

Northern Egypt's farmland has been converted from the ancient basin agriculture dependent on natural flooding and the deposit of river-borne silt, to perennial irrigation and the use of fertilizer. For thousands of years the Nile valley had remained remarkably free of the salinity problems that had plagued other systems. Now for the first time in history there is no flow of silt into the Nile Delta, and Egypt faces growing problems of salinity and waterlogging due to perennial irrigation. Downstream, where the river's flow has been slowed, salty Mediterranean waters are flooding the Nile Delta, covering thousands of acres of fertile farmland causing migrational paths of fish to be disturbed and feeding grounds altered by the loss of nutrients that formerly flowed below the dam. In recent years, the eastern Mediterranean sardine fishery has drastically declined. Behind the giant dam, chemicals used to retard evaporation in this hot, dry area may be harmful to the Lake Aswan fish that are depended upon to supply much-needed protein. Loss of the annual deposit of fertile silt on the flood plains is increasing use of chemical fertilizer, with attendant problems of pollution. The silt carried by the Nile is now accumulating in the reservoir instead.

One of the most costly and tragic side effects of the spread of modern irrigation in Egypt is the great increase in the incidence of *schistosomiasis*. This debilitating intestinal and urinary disease is produced by the parasitic larva of a blood fluke that burrows into the flesh of persons standing in ditches or water-soaked fields. Causing one out of ten deaths, *schistosomiasis* affects an estimated fifty percent of the Egyptian population. Adverse side effects of this magnitude of ecological intervention, together with Egypt's rapid population growth, have frustrated the hoped for prosperity from the billion dollar dam.

# THE HARNESSING OF ENERGY

Long after irrigation began, but certainly before 3000 B.C., man discovered a way of intervening in the energy cycle, by learning to harness animals for draft power. Using animals much stronger than himself not only augmented his own limited muscle power for tilling the soil and transport, but also enlarged his energy supply. For harnessing draft animals enabled him to convert indigestible roughage such as grass, clover, alfalfa, hay, and straw into a usable form of energy. With animal power raising the efficiency of labor, a small but significant portion of the population (around 10 percent) was freed from food production for other pursuits. Today, perhaps half the world's cropland is tilled with draft animals — cattle, buffalo, and camels. Particularly in Asia and Africa, draft animals, primarily oxen and camels, have been used throughout history for non-field farming operations such as threshing grain and turning wheels to raise water for irrigation. From the time that draft energy was originally harnessed until fossil-fuel energy was harnessed, the only other sources of power tapped for agriculture were wind and water, and their use was confined to nonfield operations, such as threshing and delivering irrigation water in specific geographical areas.

Some five thousand years after the harnessing of draft animals the development of the internal combustion engine ultimately gave man an enormous capacity to till the earth. The burning of fossil fuels permitted him to tap solar energy received by the earth centuries ago, and stored underground as petroleum. By increasing the productivity of labor employed in agriculture, burning of fossil fuels ushered in an era when a minority could feed the majority. The use of fossil fuels also enabled man to free cropland for other purposes by substituting the product of eons-old photosynthesis for the products of current photosynthesis — the oats, corn and hay grown as feed. Replacing horses with tractors in the United States between 1930 and 1950, released for other purposes 70 million acres of farmland that had been devoted to feeding horses. Acreage around the world freed by substituting tractors for horses and other draft animals would probably easily amount to a quarter of a billion acres.

The harnessing of draft animals and mechanical power enormously boosted man's capacity for expanding the food producing capacity of the earth by bringing additional land under cultivation. In the New World, pre-Columbian Indians had limited their farming largely to the rich, light alluvial soils of the river flood plains. The introduction of draft animals from Europe, together with the steel plow, opened the tough, virgin sods of the Great Plains for crop farming. Much earlier in northern Europe, draft animals, combined with improvement in harnessing and the development of communal farming, made possible the opening of vast areas of rich, heavy, wet soil. But depending on animals for draft power as well as for food opened the way to an increase in animal numbers that nearly paralleled growth in human numbers. As livestock populations increased in the more densely populated areas of the world, their grazing needs came to exceed the replenishment rate of natural vegetation, resulting in a gradual denuding of the countryside. Whole regions of the Middle East, North Africa, and Mediterranean Europe have undergone ecological transformation due to the overgrazing of man's domesticates.

Traditionally, mechanical power was thought of in connection with saving labor. But mechanical power, and to a lesser extent draft power, also raised the productivity of cropland in a number of ways: by making possible better seedbed preparation; better timing of planting, watering, harvesting and threshing; more even and effective application of pesticides; and greater opportunity for multiple cropping, particularly by providing irrigation water and shortening crop cycles. Agriculture remains a major consumer of energy in both agricultural and industrial societies. Where agriculture is highly mechanized today, the expenditure of fossil-fuel energy per acre is often substantially greater than the food energy produced on the acre. This deficit in output was of no immediate consequence as long as man could draw generously on energy in the bank, that is, in subterranean fossil-fuel deposits. The implications of scarce, tighter, costlier fossil-fuel energy supplies for energy-intensive agriculture in advanced industrial societies are not now known (Ehrlich et al.,1976). But energy accounting, in addition to financial accounting, is now being introduced into agriculture. Opportunities for conserving energy in food production are being sought and identified.

When fossil fuels eventually become scarcer, man will have to return to the more traditional forms of agriculture, relying on his own energies as well as those of his draft animals. Or, he will have to turn to some other source of motive energy for agriculture, perhaps nuclear or the direct harnessing of solar energy (Steinhart and Steinhart, 1974). To date, harnessing large power supplies directly from solar energy appears technologically unpromising. Very little nuclear energy is used at present to produce food, except in the few areas where nuclear plants are providing electricity for milking cows or heating poultry houses. No field-tillage operations are fueled by nuclear energy thus far, since there is not yet an efficient means of converting it into mobile form.

## OLD AND NEW WORLD CROP AND LIVESTOCK EXCHANGE

Columbus profoundly affected the earth's food-producing capacity at the end of the fifteenth century when he linked the formerly independent systems of the Old and New World agricultures and set in motion an exchange of crops and animals among various parts of the world. This exchange has greatly enlarged the earth's capacity to sustain growing human populations on all continents. Many transported crops turned out to be better suited for their new ecological niches than their areas of origin.Furthermore, large stretches of land became more productive with introduced crops. Without the small grains of wheat, rye, barley, and oats, much of the vast lower rainfall regions in the United States would have remained as grassland. Corn, the only indigenous New World grain, required more moisture than is commonly available over a large part of the Great Plains and elsewhere.

The introduction of the potato from South America into China and northern Europe greatly augmented their food supply. The Irish population grew rapidly for several decades, and only when the potato crop was devastated by blight was population growth actually checked. Unknown in the Old World before Columbus, corn is now grown on every continent, is widely used as animal feed, and is one of the world's three principal grain staples. Introduced from China several decades ago, the soybean is the leading United States source of vegetable oil and is the principal farm export. Grain sorghum, stored aboard early slave ships, crossed the Atlantic from Africa as a source of food. Today, it is the second-ranking feed grain in the United States. The sunflower, also a crop domesticated by pre-Columbian Indians is still growing wild on the Great Plains, and is the principal source of vegetable oil for the Soviet Union. The exchange of crops between the two worlds was very much two-way; but this was not originally the case with livestock. The New World is indebted to the Old for all its livestock and poultry species, with the exception of the turkey, the Muscovy duck, the guinea pig, llama and alpaca. Remarkable progress in genetics and breeding have made America the leading international source of livestock as breeding animals. The movement of crops and animals between the two worlds continues as the nature of the crops changes through genetic manipulation, as environments are altered, and as these two factors interact with the changing demands of the marketplace. Contemporary technological developments, such as the launching of earth-circling resource satellites, promise to further the rational matching of crops to growing environments.

## AGRICHEMICALS

The development of agricultural chemicals has produced powerful tools for intervening in the earth's ecosystem and expanding its food-yielding capacity. Literally hundreds of chemical compounds are used in modern agriculture to control weeds and pests and fertilize the soil.

Justus von Liebig, the nineteenth-century German chemist, is known as the father of soil chemistry. By identifying the importance of the major plant growth nutrients — particularly nitrogen, phosphorus, and potassium — and demonstrating that the soil's natural fertility could be restored or enhanced by adding these nutrients in proper proportions, von Liebig laid the groundwork for chemical fertilizer use. Land resources in much of the world at that time still gave ample opportunity to plow up more land to meet expanding food needs. It was not until the disappearance of most frontiers in the twentieth century that use of chemical fertilizers became widespread, as farmers eventually learned to substitute fertilizer for land. By the mid-1970s the world's farmers were using roughly 80 million metric tons of plant nutrients on 3.6 billion acres of cropland — about 50 pounds per acre.

Chemical fertilizer usage varies widely among countries and geographic regions, with more intensive usage in densely populated industrial countries located in high rainfall, temperate regions, while in some poor countries, chemical fertilizers are scarcely used. Japan practices intensive agriculture and applies chemical fertilizers at a rate of more than 300 pounds per acre yearly. If chemical fertilizers were discontinued, soil fertility would decline rapidly, dropping food production by perhaps half or more. If usage were discontinued on a global basis, the human food supply would probably drop by at least one-fourth (Brown and Finsterbusch, 1972).

Historically, leguminous plants such as clover were included in agricultural rotation schemes to periodically boost the soil's nitrogen content. In nature, bacteria in the soil, the best known of which are the nitrogen-fixing bacteria associated with root nodules of leguminous plants, change gaseous nitrogen into an assimilable form. Gaseous nitrogen, abundant in the atmosphere, is not assimilable by higher plants and animals although both require nitrogen. Synthesis of atmospheric nitrogen into inorganic compounds in the current century, however, has made possible low-cost nitrogen fertilizers, such as *ammonium sulfate* or *ammonium nitrate*, making nitrogen fertilizer application more economic than using clover, alfalfa, or soybeans in rotation. The planetary nitrogen supply is seemingly limitless, but its "mining" requires large energy inputs.

Potassium reserves in Canada's rich potash fields alone are estimated to meet world needs for several centuries. Phosphorus, however, is the least plentiful nutrient and could become a constraining factor in food production. Around 3.5 million tons of it wash into the ocean each year from the earth's land masses. If there is to be a great demand for the mining of nutrients from the ocean bed, the economic pressures to mine phosphorus might be among the earlier ones to develop.

Chemical fertilizers have greatly benefited humanity, and their use is bound to increase, although it is resulting in disturbing ecological problems, which will be discussed later. This is unfortunate since there is no viable alternative to fertilizers yet available for increasing food production. Recycled organic wastes from humans, animals, and plants cannot be substituted for chemical nutrients; however, more efficient use of them is filling some portion of the need. These organic fertilizers have the ecological benefits of improving soil structure and reducing soil erosion and chemical fertilizer runoff.

In the modern era, chemical pesticide use, added to millennia-old ways of protecting and favoring domesticated species, has become widespread in the twentieth century, increasing rapidly since World War II. Chemical control has contributed greatly to intensified agriculture and expanded food supplies. While the chemical control of pests has had an enormous impact on the size and quality of the human food supply, no one knows how to reliably estimate its contribution. Test plot results show dramatic yields associated with pesticides in the United States and elsewhere, but the gain varies with the crops and the locations. Older simpler pesticides such as arsenic, and compounds containing lead, mercury, or copper have been used for almost a century. With the introduction and spread of synthetic pesticides in the past quarter-century or so, particularly the chlorinated hydrocarbons of which DDT is one, numerous and far-reaching environmental consequences have begun to appear. Though cheaper to manufacture, these synthetics do not break down or decompose readily in nature. They are highly toxic and capable of affecting a broad range of life beyond the pest target. They are also highly mobile, circulating widely in water and air currents. The long-term consequences of these accumulating nondegradable pesticides in the biosphere are not known. But it is clear that the use of DDT and other chlorinated hydrocarbons is beginning to threaten many species of animal life, including man.

# SELECTIVE BREEDING AND GENETICS

Man's intervention in the natural cycles of plant and animal species has altered their genetic composition and greatly increased their productivity and his own food supply. By changing other characteristics as well, specific foods were created from various strains to suit human desires. Even before Gregor Mendel's discovery of the fundamental principles of heredity, the genetic composition of domesticated species was remarkably rearranged, improved through the selecting and favoring of desired strains throughout millennia and centuries. The extraordinary development of corn by New World Indians is a case in point. Not only did American Indians eventually enlarge strawberry-size corn ears containing only eight rows of forty to fifty kernels each to more productive ears measuring six to eight inches with seventeen rows and many more kernels; but, from an original Central American domesticate, they differentiated and developed varieties that could survive and flourish in an amazing variety of North and South American soils, climates, and habitats.

The discoveries of genetics have given man a great boost in his breeding efforts, enabling the development of remarkably productive and adaptive new breeds in relatively short periods of time. For example, hybrid corn, with increased yields and short growing seasons, has extended the northern limit of commercial corn growing in the United States some 500 miles. Through advances in breeding and feeding man has achieved impressive results in his efforts to increase the productivity of domesticated animals. The early ancestors of our current hen probably did not lay more than one clutch of about fifteen eggs per year. Over a period of time man worked to increase this egg-laying capacity, using decoys in nests to foster the nesting instinct and coax the hen to produce more than the normal clutch. Today the nesting instinct has been bred out of chickens in many parts of the world. American hens lay an average of 228 eggs yearly now and the number is rising. An industrious Japanese hen holds the world record, having laid 365 eggs in one year.

Early domesticates of the cow probably did not produce more than 600 pounds of milk per year, the average amount of milk produced by cows in India today and barely enough to support a calf to the point where it could forage for itself. In antiquity, often a decoy calf (a man dressed in hides) was used to encourage a cow to lactate when it was not nursing a calf. Through centuries of discovering, selecting, and breeding better strains, the gradual development of dairy cows enabled much more milk to be produced than necessary to sustain a calf for the year intended by nature. Modern dairy cows in the United States produce ten thousand pounds of milk per year, or almost seventeen times the amount produced by their ancestors. Recently a Washington state cow, Skagvale Grateful Hattie, produced a new world record of forty-four thousand pounds of milk in a 365 day period. This amounts to fifty-five quarts daily or seventy times more than her predecessors.

An historic breakthrough was recently accomplished by plant breeders in creating the new high-yielding varieties of wheat and rice for tropical and semitropical areas of the earth. In the tropics, traditional cereal varieties are the result of millennia of natural selection. Strains that survived are those capable of competing with weeds for sunlight and withstanding heavy tropical rain and floods. The result has been tall, thin plants able to keep their heads above water and in the sun. These traditional plants are not highly responsive to fertilizer. When fertilized liberally, the plants become top-heavy with grain and fall over or lodge before the grain is ripe, causing heavy losses. The key to the productivity of the new varieties is their fertilizer responsiveness. Plant breeders redesigned the wheat and rice plants, producing plants with short, stiff straw stems that stand up under the weight of heavier yields. The old long-strawed varieties were able to absorb only about forty pounds of nitrogen per acre before yields began to decline as a result of lodging. The new dwarf varieties can take three times as much fertilizer.

The new varieties also use fertilizer more efficiently, producing more grain per pound. Thus, a given level of production can be reached with them using far less fertilizer. In fact, the new plants are more efficient users of water, land, and labor as well. They are aseasonal, that is, not extremely sensitive to variations in photoperiod, giving them great adaptability to different seasons of the year and to a wide range of differing geographical locations. Through millennia of selection, traditional varieties in given locales are very sensitive to daylength. They have become responsive to and dependent upon specific seasonal cycles and can be planted only at a certain time of year — at the onset of the monsoon season, for example. Many of the new varieties also mature early, opening up fresh possibilities for multiple cropping. IR-8, the most productive new rice variety, is ready for harvest in four months, while local varieties take five or six months.

Corn's protein quality is traditionally limited by deficiencies in the essential amino acids, *tryptophan* and *lysine*. The discovery at Purdue University in 1963 of a high-lysine gene in a collection of corn germ plasm opened a new door in the effort to combat global protein malnutrition, particularly in large corn-eating regions of Latin America and sub-Saharan Africa. By 1969, commercial corn varieties with high-lysine content were released, but this genetic breakthrough has other ecological implications. For where the new corn is used as livestock feed, costly protein supplements could be substantially reduced, thus relieving pressure on agricultural resources. While enormously increasing the productivity of a given species, little success has been made in creating new species. Since 1888 plant breeders have known about *triticale*, a cross between wheat and rye, first bred in Germany with exceptionally high protein yield. Recently, highly fertile and superior grains of wheat and rye have been discovered. If these two characteristics can be combined, *triticale* may soon be competitive with established cereals. Exciting possibilities of developing other man-made cereals also exist. A great dream of plant engineers today is the creation, through direct joining of cells, of cereal varieties with the nitrogen-fixing properties of legumes (Brown and Finsterbusch, 1972).

Agriculture, in simplest terms, was an effort by man to shape the environment to better suit his needs. By singling out and favoring a handful of crops and animals that in the wild had served as sources of food and clothing, protecting them and discriminating against their competitors, he altered the relative abundance and distribution of the world's plant and animal life. Man and his domesticates were eventually to dominate the earth. Not only was man to dominate nature, he was also to shape, mold, transform, and affect, at an accelerating rate, most living and nonliving things; not just for his "own" time, but for millennia to come. Man-the-tiller had developed a seemingly endless capacity for intervening in and altering his environment. In terms of changing the face of the earth, the agricultural intervention, so far, is unparalleled.

The great achievements of cultivation and husbandry created a more abundant and secure food supply, allowing man to break out of the limits on number and density (and lifestyle) set by unmanaged nature. This made possible an immediate and continuing increase in his numbers, and in the size and number of agricultural villages replacing nomad camps. The remarkable growth in population attending the initial enlargement of the food supply was a virtual demographic revolution. Agriculture established the basis for permanent settlement and civilization. As agricultural techniques extended and became more efficient, the earth's food producing capacity continually expanded. Gains in food production permitted human numbers to increase. These increases absorbed the additional food in turn, exerting pressure on the food supply, thus providing powerful incentives to devise still more efficient means of producing food. Population growth and advances in food production have dynamically reinforced each other and brought man to the place where he wishes to moderate the cycle before agricultural stresses on the earth's ecosystem become too great. For while interventions in nature for food were initially simple and limited to a few small areas of the planet, they became successively more complex and widespread. Eventually some of their consequences were to exceed understanding, thereby creating worrisome problems. Today the more serious problems are global in scale. The pressures for increased food production through mounting population and rising affluence remain strong. Moreover, hunger and malnutrition remain the lot of a large segment of mankind, suggesting that expanding food production alone is not enough.

Social and cultural evolution had occurred incredibly slow while man was a hunter. But after perhaps 4 million years of wandering and preying upon the environment, a step was taken with the domestication and control of food sources that enabled him to go from the cave to the moon in a mere twelve thousand years. Certainly the evolution of civilization would have been impossible without the enlargement of the human food supply through the conscious control of plants and animals. Even if the achievement of agriculture did not predetermine them, subsequent developments quickly followed. It is no coincidence that the invention of agriculture and the rise of early civilizations occurred within a few thousand years of each other. In a hunting society, very few were freed from the quest for food. The ability to produce and store food in granaries and on the hoof released some people, albeit a small minority at first, from the incessant search for sustenance. Agriculture eventually made possible the formation of cities, removing older limits to social change. Grain fields and herds fed the populations of the earliest urban cities of Catal Huyuk and Jericho (7000 B.C.). Later, the growing urban populations of the Tigris-Euphrates and Nile valleys were fed by grain fields and herds, sometime after 4000 B.C. Still later they supported early cities on Crete, in the Indus Valley of western India, in the Yellow River valley, and more recently in the New World.

Although the surplus of food was never large, agricultural workers were able to produce more than they required. This surplus was used to support specialists in other occupations — artisans, priests, soldiers, toolmakers, officials — and used also, to a limited degree, for trade. Organized projects such as the building of roads, temples, irrigation canals, and harbors were carried out. As agriculture advanced over the centuries, more and more men were freed from the land. Newer centers of commerce and learning sprang up. Eventually, the Industrial Revolution and modern society emerged, able to feed whole populations with less than 5 percent tilling the land. Yet for millennia *after* the agricultural intervention began, most people spent most of their time in the quest for food, living on the land in small settlements where the work was. Largely because of the limitation on energy sources known and exploited, most of mankind could afford to satisfy only the more elementary biological (subsistence) needs — the necessities of life: food, clothing, shelter, — and at rather minimal or unsatisfactory levels. Life expectancy in the agricultural era remained universally low, mass transportation was generally nonexistent, and all communications were costly and insecure. The lifting of these harsh constraints and the beginning of substantial changes in the conditions and prospects of human life remained for the next era in the interaction between humans and earth.

# 3  The Industrial Era

The Industrial Revolution was a great change in the means of production, which occurred in England approximately 200 years ago. It radically changed man's relation to the environment by magnifying enormously his capacity for intervening in the natural system. It ushered in a new era in the relationship between humans and earth; an era that has recently, a mere two centuries later, ended. It was an era of abundance and promise. The supply of energy, raw materials, and other resources seemed endless. With the substitution of mineral for vegetable or animal substances, man was no longer restricted mainly to subsistence conditions and the current agricultural output for the satisfaction of his needs (Brown, 1972; McNeill, 1965).

## RAPID TECHNOLOGICAL ADVANCE

The abundance and variety of mutually reinforcing technological advances associated with and flowing from the Industrial Revolution, including new ways of organizing production, defy compilation. At the heart of the industrial intervention was a new capacity for intervening in the earth's energy cycle through machines that harnessed vast stores of fossil fuels hidden for eons in the earth's crust. This new intervention opened for use what appeared to be a limitless supply of cheap energy in the earth's ecosystem. The enormous convenience of such energy is more fully appreciated as it is becoming all too "scarce." Fossil fuels are a form of solar energy resulting from past photosynthesis, which are mobile, storable, and easily adaptable to a wide range of agricultural and industrial operations. Tapping them enabled man to move beyond the muscle power of the horse, mule, ox, camel, or llama, and beyond the limited harnessing of wind and water power.

First, the steam engine called for coal and later the internal combustion engine required petroleum. More and more human tasks were performed by machines fueled by inanimate energy sources. Today, coal, oil, and other raw materials are gathered from the earth at breakneck speeds with no end in view, transforming the earth in the process. Advancing technology has also enabled the intervention in and the enlarged use of other natural systems and resources, i.e., the earth's hydrologic system, its climate system, its waste absorptive capacity, and its oceans.

The industrial intervention spread from England to other European countries after 1830. It expanded to North America following the Civil War, then to Japan in the early twentieth century. It is still affecting agriculture and industry on all continents, transforming human society and the material conditions of life widespread. The world became obsessed with the effort to industrialize and grow in material affluence, and exponentially advancing technology made it possible. The unfolding agricultural intervention opened the way for more rapid economic, social, and cultural development than had the prior 4 million years of hunting and gathering. It was still very slow, however, compared to the rapid and manifold change that was to come with the industrial era and the enlarging human capacity to intervene in the environment.

Rapid advances in all kinds of technology, based on the systematic development and application of knowledge to practical tasks, characterize the whole industrial era, starting with that seemingly miraculous improvement in the tools of production two centuries ago. Those new revolutionary processes seemed to their originators to be simply practical solutions to practical problems, devoid of wide social significance. But rapid technological advance fed back and reinforced an upward cycle of technical expansion. This upward cycle has been reinforced by specialization and division of labor in science and technology, and by the systematic investment in technological growth through steadily expanding research and development (R & D) expenditures. In 1930 the world was spending almost a billion dollars on R & D. Since 1940, the absolute amount and the share of the gross global product invested in the generation of new knowledge has risen astronomically. By the early 1970s, an estimated $70 billion or 2.6 percent of the gross global product (of nearly $3 trillion) was invested annually in R & D. Most of this investment and growth was confined to the rich countries, such as the United States in which R & D expenditures in 1970 were $27 billion or nearly 40 percent of the world total. Worldwide, most R & D expenditures were directed toward military-related research, particularly new weapons research, followed by nuclear and space research.

Accelerating technological advance is so fundamental to industrial intervention that Alfred North Whitehead called the greatest invention of the industrial era "the invention of invention itself." The growing specialization and division of labor in industrial society, facilitated by man's enlarged productive capacities, eventually resulted in the separation of those who developed new technologies from those who applied and are responsible for new technologies. This institutional and often geographic distance contributed to technology's increasing independence and autonomous force in modern society. Technology is broadly defined here to include man's ability to organize production units and markets. This "softer" technology was evident early in large group-hunting endeavors, organized irrigation projects, and the building of pyramids. But with the advancement in communications and transportation, there was a takeoff in the ability to coordinate larger and more complex human undertakings and organizations. This softer technology is by no means less significant than technologies of a more physical character, such as the ability to spin synthetic fibers or plant rice from airplanes. It is simply less visible and measurable. Prior to the industrial era a shop or a farm which employed more than a few hundred people was rare. With the coming of new forms of business organizations such as industrial factories, the size of economic units enlarged both in the number of employees and in the value of output. In the latter years industrial growth expanded dramatically, exceeding in some cases several billion dollars of output per year and a million employees. Today literally hundreds of corporations around the world have more than ten thousand employees. Many multinational corporations exceed the size of national states, the characteristic political unit of the industrial era.

Accompanying the change in relation to the environment, the size of basic political units increased as well. From the tribe of the hunting era, society progressed to the village and city state of the agricultural era to the nation state of the industrial era. Although attempts to unify people into a nation state with a specified territory reaches back at least two millennia (China unified in 220 B.C.), the emergence of the nation state as the characteristic political organization awaited the industrial era. It was only in the last decades of the era, with the dismantling of European colonial empires, that the whole of humankind became divided into sovereign nation states. Yet the world, as we shall see, is already moving willy-nilly toward a more integrated global society with new global institutions.

In the preagricultural and agricultural eras, human energies and efforts were centered nearly exclusively on the perennial quest for food. In contrast, as the industrial era unfolded, a growing proportion of concern and energy moved into the production of a profusion of other goods and services. But food production was and remained the basis of it all. Agriculture fathered the Industrial Revolution which, once underway, fed back and magnified agricultural intervention. Fossil-fuel energy was harnessed for cultivating fields and performing other farm operations. New technologies and the expansion of industrial and service sectors of modern societies gave agriculture an enormous array of resources essential to keep food production in line with expanding food needs. The extent to which modern agriculture depends upon the non-agricultural sector for inputs to "make two blades of grass grow where one once grew" underlines the contribution of the Industrial Revolution. Materials purchased by American farmers totaled more than $21 billion in 1970. Japanese farmers, with a high-rainfall rice culture and a more intensive mode of cultivation, spent even more per acre than their American counterparts. Techniques for processing, preserving, storing, and transporting food, increased the quantity and quality of the diet, particularly in rich countries. Plowing up more land and raising yields on land already under cultivation are two major ways to expand the food supply. During the time that agriculture has been practiced, increases in the world food supply have come largely from expanding cultivated area. As cultivation moved from valley to valley, continent to continent, and as populations increased, more land was plowed. Globally and throughout history, increases in yields per acre were scarcely perceptible within any given generation. Only during the twentieth century did countries achieve rapid and continuing increases in output per acre, culminating in a midcentury global turning point. Since 1950, increases in the world's food supply have come more from raising yields on the existing cultivated areas than from expanding the area cultivated. At present, perhaps as much as 80 percent of food increase comes from the former.

In coaxing significantly higher yields from an acre of land, man applied on a commercial basis the technologies developed earlier in the industrial era — plant breeding, agricultural chemistry, mechanization, and advanced irrigation. Industrialization and the twentieth-century agricultural revolution proceeded side by side in Japan, which made the transition around the turn of the century. This archipelagic country was already densely populated and turned to the oceans for protein. The limited land was used for producing starchy staples, principally rice, to meet growing food energy needs. The typical Japanese fish and rice diet has its roots in this population-land crisis. A few densely populated European nations, including the Netherlands and Denmark, also achieved yield takeoffs around the same time.

Near midcentury, another group of countries including the United States and the United Kingdom made the transition. These were economically advanced countries with either much arable land in relation to population or with national policies that discriminated against agriculture while developing industry. England had placed priorities on developing industry and exporting manufactured goods in exchange for foodstuffs and raw materials. Population growth had characterized Britain, but large numbers had migrated to other parts of the world. Improvements in agriculture centered on mechanization and were designed mainly to save labor, not to raise the productivity of land. It took the U-boat threat during World War II to spur the United Kingdom to intensify cultivation sufficiently to generate a yield takeoff. The United States tried for two and a half decades after the closing of the frontier in 1915 to make the transition to the yield-raising method of increasing food output. Finally, per acre crop yields began to rise around 1940, and have continued upward. The American yield takeoff was, in the broadest sense, the result of a massive application of accumulated scientific knowledge and technology to agriculture. Despite the midcentury global transition, advanced farm technologies were confined mainly to the rich industrial countries and to plantation and export crops elsewhere. This caused widespread concern because, in the decades following World War II, Malthusian forces were vigorously at work in the poor countries. Death rates dropped with the spread of modern medicine and sanitation, while birth rates did not. Consequently, population growth rates soared far above any experienced by the newly industrialized countries. Without the vast frontiers of fertile, well-watered land that could quickly and cheaply be brought under the plow, and lacking the technologies to raise yields, all but a few of the poor countries were transformed from food exporters into food importers between 1945 and 1965. An agricultural breakthrough in the poor countries awaited the green revolution of the late 1960s, which was essentially the spread of the twentieth-century agricultural revolution into the southern part of the planet.

The green revolution is the shorthand expression for the introduction and rapid spread of new high-yielding wheat and rice breeds. Given proper management and the necessary fertilizer and water, they actually double yields (Dalrymple, 1974). They are the product of the first systematic attempt to develop agricultural technology, designed specifically to take advantage of the unique growing conditions of the tropics and the subtropics, particularly their wealth of solar energy. The wheats, which came first, were developed over a score of years in Mexico by American scientists. The rices came later, and faster, mainly through work at the International Rice Research Institute in the Philippines. Due to their high-yield capacity the new grains have spread rapidly in the poor countries, particularly in Asia. Between 1965 and 1975 the area expanded from 200 acres to more than 80 million acres. Country after country reported unprecedented cereal production increases in the late 1960s. West Pakistan's wheat production jumped 70 percent between 1967 and 1969, a most remarkable upward leap, making that country a net exporter in the late sixties. India more than doubled its wheat production between 1965 and 1971, bringing itself to the threshold of self-sufficiency by 1972 — just before another cycle of poor weather affected the monsoon belt, followed by sharply rising fertilizer and fuel prices. The Philippines ended more than half a century of dependence on rice imports, only to again need food aid in the early 1970s due to civil disorder. Ceylon's rice harvest increased by a third in two years. Takeoffs in wheat yields per acre on the Indo-Pakistan subcontinent following the introduction of the new wheats made the earlier corn-yield takeoff in the United States or the rice-yield takeoff in Japan seem mild by comparison.

Despite increased output from the green revolution, nutritional deficit remains a fact of life in much of the underdeveloped world, even in countries reaching economic self-sufficiency in cereals. The great mass of people in these countries do not have incomes high enough to obtain enough of the right foods. Overcoming hunger and feeding future populations will involve far more than simply expanding the food supply. The green revolution temporarily arrested the deteriorating food situation in such populous countries as India, Pakistan, Indonesia, Turkey, and the Philippines. Lifting the threat of famine for the time being, it provided a breathing space to slow population growth and find ways to offset some of the adverse consequences of expanding agricultural intervention into the earth's ecosystem. Already, some are saying that the time which was bought was an opportunity lost. The population of the world, especially the less-developed countries, continues to explode.

# POPULATION EXPLOSION AND URBANIZATION

The change in relation between man and environment brought by the industrial era opened the door to a massive rise in human numbers, a virtual explosion of population in the twentieth century. By 1975 more than 4 billion people inhabited the earth. Population was increasing beyond historical precedent, at just under 2 percent per year, adding approximately 80 million people, enough to create a new nation. In the 4 million year preagricultural era, human numbers did not exceed 10 million. The 12 thousand year agricultural period saw a very slow but gradual acceleration in the population growth rate, after an initial burst at its start. As population increased, agricultural innovation increased also, setting in motion a mutually reinforcing cycle that continues today. Nevertheless, the net increase in numbers was so slow, a mere 3 percent per century, that it was imperceptible within a given generation. By the start of the industrial era, world population had not yet reached one billion, and growth was centered in Europe and Asia. By creating new economic opportunities and industrial advances that further increased the human food supply, the Industrial Revolution accelerated world population growth; and by 1860 it had reached 1 billion. Yet few countries had ever experienced a rate of natural increase beyond 1 percent per year.

Population growth occurs when births exceed deaths. For the most part, world population increase has occurred because the death rate has *decreased*, not because the birth rate has increased. The burst of scientific, technological, and economic activity and ingenuity following World War II contributed substantially to the earth's food-producing capacity and improved dramatically man's capacity to control diseases. As death rates plummeted, creating an imbalance unlike any before, populations began to increase at an explosive rate, particularly in the developing countries that had not experienced the demographic transition to lowered birth rates that occurred with the industrialization and urbanization of rich countries. In some countries the yearly rate of population increase is between 3 and 4 percent. This twentieth-century explosion in human growth is a profound phenomenon. Yet, there are now indications as we shall see later, that the long-term trend of demographic growth, beginning as recently in history as the agricultural era, rising rapidly and on a worldwide basis during the industrial era, may be approaching an end. Besides growth in simple numbers, industrialization meant a shift of the population toward urban centers (Davis, 1971). Agriculture released a small minority from the land and the perennial quest for food, but efficient harnessing of inanimate energy sources in the industrial era permitted the productivity of agricultural labor to multiply dozens of times. In the twentieth century, less than 5 percent of the population can feed an entire advanced society. This increased efficiency opened the way for the large-scale movement of people from countryside to city.

Technological advances in agriculture permitted urban centers to emerge millennia ago. But in even the largest settlements such as Mesopotamia, Egypt's Nile valley, the Indus valley, Persia, and Greece, urban populations probably numbered less than two hundred thousand inhabitants (only 1 to 2 percent of the total population at best). Exceptions were ancient Rome and seventeenth-century London, cities which had reached at least a million inhabitants. Urbanization had proceeded very slowly up until 1800 where in the New World, only Philadelphia and New York had as many as thirty-five thousand inhabitants. Of the American population 95 percent lived in communities of no more than

2,500. In Europe, people on the whole were overwhelmingly agrarian, with only 22 percent of the population living in cities of one hundred thousand or more. The great divergence between rural and urban modes of life is also a product of the industrial era. In the agricultural era, towns were merely centers of trade, religion, learning, and other cultural activities in a more complex but basically agricultural world.

As the Industrial Revolution unfolded, urbanization progressed rapidly in Western Europe. In 1800, for example, less than one-tenth of the population of England and Wales lived in cities of one hundred thousand or larger. By 1900 the majority of the population was urban, and Great Britain was the only society that could be regarded as predominantly urban. By 1970 all the industrial, rich, northern hemisphere nations were highly urbanized. Today more than one-third of all mankind lives in urban areas, and urbanization is rapidly accelerating.

Urbanization, the movement from countryside to city, is a finite process. Some societies have reached a point of stability, with the urban share of the total population approximately 80 percent. That is not to say the total urban population or particular urban areas have stopped growing in size, but that the urban share of population tends not to increase beyond that point. England has already reached such "urban maturity," while several northern European industrial societies, including West Germany, the Netherlands, and Belgium, are approaching it. The United States with 75 percent urban is not far from it.

Urbanization is occurring in most rich industrial countries and in all developing countries. In the poor countries, urbanization differs from the industrial societies by the sheer size of the migration. The projected migration for Latin America, Asia, and Africa promises to be the largest in history. The scale of past waves of migration—-from Europe to America, or from the North American east coast westward—did not even remotely approach the massive rural urban migration now underway. The rate of transition from rural to urban settlement and society in the poor countries is also unprecedented. Urban populations in the poor countries now total 800 million and may quadruple by the year 2000, but the total population is doubling approximately every twenty-five years. In many slums and shantytowns, it is doubling in five to seven years. By 2000 the urban share of the total population of Asia, Africa and Latin America is expected to reach 42 percent and increase rapidly thereafter (Beir et al., 1975). The cities of these poor countries are not ready for this influx. Rapid urbanization is running ahead of industrialization and significant economic growth. Nineteenth- and twentieth-century industrial centers of Europe and America with their need for labor, in effect pulled people from farm into the city. Today people pushed out of the countryside in Asia, Latin America, and Africa by uncontrolled population growth and lack of opportunity are moving, without jobs, filling urban slums, forming ghettos of unemployment and poverty beyond imagination. Urbanization is not inherently destructive to the environment, but there have always been various kinds of environmental problems associated with it. Today the concentration of activities in dense urban populations is adversely affecting both natural and man-made ecosystems, destroying landscapes, and undermining human habitats. The waste absorptive capacity of the air, the water, and the land systems are overloaded, and even climate has been locally and regionally changed. Since in poor countries resources, technology, and capital are scarce, massive rural-urban migration is making it difficult to provide even basic amenities. For example, two decades of exploding population growth in West Bengal, increased the pressure on the land to the point where literally millions of Bengalis had neither land nor the prospect of enough employment in the countryside to ward off starvation (Brown, 1974). They were driven by desperation to Calcutta where 50 percent of the families now live in one room, including at least one hundred thousand people living on the sidewalks. Not only do new urban immigrants have insufficient space and housing, they lack even more rudimentary services and amenities such as clean water and air. Latin America's number one environmental problem is enlarging urban populations that are destroying the landscape and polluting water systems with human sewage. Since urban facilities are already overburdened, the level of services will probably deteriorate in principal urban centers in the absence of massive external assistance.

While there has been a move to less dense living in the trek to the suburbs in the rich countries, in the developing countries there is no place for urban poor to go. For the first time in history, there are no frontiers in most of the world (Murdoch, 1975). Little exists in past human experience with which to understand the social repercussions of this rural-urban migration in the poor countries. This is not to say that urbanization in the poor countries should be viewed in a totally negative light. Economic and social opportunities are still greater in the cities, but the risk is that Calcutta could become the model city of the future. Lack of steady employment for the great majority of slum and shantytown dwellers is reportedly causing pervasive alienation and despair. Exposure of these people to better living conditions elsewhere within the same city and, through communications media, in the rest of the world, when their own prospects for improvement are limited, could be creating potentially disruptive conditions. There are ninety cities in 1975 in the developing world alone with populations of over a million. By the year 2000 nearly 300 such cities are projected (Beir et al., 1975). There are now more than a dozen urban centers in the world with more than eight million population, including Calcutta, Peking, Shanghai, Mexico City, Buenos Aires, São Paulo, and Rio de Janiero. Individual cities have not only grown larger but have tended to flow together into urban *megalopolises*. The Greek planner, Constantine Doxiadis, identified the following megalopolitan areas in the world: Eastern United States (Boston / Washington D.C.); The Great Lakes (Detroit / Chicago); California (Los Angeles / San Diego); Japan (Tokyo / Yokohama, Osaka / Kobe); China (Shanghai / Nanking, Peking / Tientsin, Hong Kong / Canton); Indonesia (Djakarta / Bandoeng); Egypt (Cairo / Alexandria); The Rhine (Amsterdam / The Hague, Cologne / Dortmund); England (London / Manchester) and Italy (Milan / Turin). If present trends continue, in the twentieth century human society will be transfomed from a primarily rural to a primarily urban society. The human habitat is becoming rapidly man-made with human beings in close and continuous contact with other human beings, involving a degree of social complexity unknown before.

# THE PURSUIT OF MATERIAL ABUNDANCE

Man's new productive capacity ushered in an era of rapid and self-sustaining economic growth. Wherever industry took hold, an unprecedented increase occurred in per capita productivity. For the first time in history, incomes and living standards began to rise for a large and growing minority. Previously, technological advances that ameliorated the human condition by an increase in agricultural output had always been followed by an increase in population that absorbed the gains—as is still true in developing countries today. Now both technological advance and economic activity were growing fast enough to generate an enlarging surplus which in turn facilitated a greater division of human labor and specialization and generated a continuing flow of investment and technological innovation. Thus, Malthus, writing near the start of the industrial era, had not seen the full power of industrial technology to change human material conditions and human perceptions, values, and aspirations. The ceiling of Malthus's positive or natural checks—food supply, pestilence, war—on human population growth was lifted, and the discussion of the human carrying capacity of the planet moved out of a subsistence level framework.

Prior to the industrial era, perceived needs for most of mankind were those basic necessities for survival—food, shelter, clothing, warmth. They were destined to live in poverty and accepted it. Only a small ruling class of people had emerged with an expanded set of needs, aspirations, and expectations. If man had remained a creature with simple subsistent needs and expectations subsequent to the industrial intervention, the earth presumably would be able to sustain much larger human numbers. But he did not, and showed a seemingly limitless capacity to expand his needs and expectations. The industrial era gave a glimpse of the cornucopia. No longer was material poverty accepted and subsistent existence for mankind inevitable or necessary. Man's needs and aspirations were continuously redefined, set toward moving targets, with no limit in view. A revolution of rising expectations and aspirations became widespread, and the drive toward a higher material quality of life fueled inventions, productive activities, and interventions in the environment.

The industrial era did not do this all at once. Machines had been turned on but, across the earth, the majority of mankind remained in grinding poverty. Modern affluent man's desires are myriad, for not only did the quality of diet for the mass of people in industrial societies improve, but clothing and housing as well. Moreover, expenditures on these items decreased as a percentage of total private market basket. New categories such as health, transportation, education, recreation, entertainment, travel, were added and a host of items in each category. To his aspirations for material improvement, man added his willingness to expend his energies. As of the 1970s, the goals of continuous economic growth and ever-rising standards of living had become the global norm (Holdren and Ehrlich, 1971). For the more narrow quest for food man had substituted the quest for material abundance. Only today is the relation between material affluence and well-being seriously questioned. More visible and worrisome signs of stress on the ecosystem resulting from man's levels of economic activity and environmental intervention, and the growing sensitivity to the vast differences in levels of living between the rich and poor nations are two reasons. New energy sources, the manipulation of materials, and the protection and modification of plants and animals have immeasurably lessened the concentration of human effort on food production, reduced the crushing burden of physical labor, and freed humans for other pursuits. It has extended to millions a wealth of income and opportunity formerly enjoyed by the smallest elite. In the mid-1970s, an adequate diet was assured to most of that quarter or so of mankind living in the rich industrial societies of North America, Western and Eastern Europe, Australia, and Japan. Except for comparatively small portions of the populations on marginal incomes, the people of these rich countries now have a more than adequate diet, and many are overfed. Diets also appear now to be nutritionally adequate for virtually all of Eastern Asia, including China, North and South Korea, Taiwan, Hong Kong, Singapore, and Malaysia. Never before has such a large portion of mankind been so well fed and secure in relation to the food supply. For throughout man's existence, most of the human race has been hungry, at least seasonally if not in a chronic sense, and plagued with famine. Fully reliable and precise data are not available, but more than two-thirds of humans living today may have nutritionally adequate diets, although in most places they are not nearly as rich in livestock products as in North America and Europe (Brown, 1974; Brubaker, 1972; and Paddock and Paddock, 1967). Although perhaps a billion or more people are malnourished in Asia, Africa, and Latin America it is no longer a vast southern area of unrelieved hunger. But these advances may be threatened by new global food insecurities, particularly in the face of continuing population growth. It should be noted also that if one were to add overnutrition, the form of malnutrition most prevalent in affluent societies, the number of malnourished humans would be far greater.

By the end of the industrial era, life expectancy at birth had climbed to close to seventy years in most northern temperate zone industrial countries. Latin America and several East Asian populations reached a life expectancy of sixty years. In Africa, the Middle East and the Indian-Pakistan subcontinent, life expectancy is still low—just over fifty years in India, barely forty years in a number of African nations. Over the past few decades, the share of the population that is literate has increased, but the total number of illiterates has also increased due to rapid growth. In the last two decades of the industrial era, literacy levels moved up slowly in Latin America and rapidly in East Asia. But again, Africa, the Middle East, and the Indian-Pakistan subcontinent contain the largest number of illiterates. While at the beginning of the era an increase in population was highly welcomed as a benefit, toward the end, it was of growing concern. The global population growth rate probably peaked just over 2 percent at some time in the late 1960s. By the early 1970s, it was below 1.9 percent, but the celebration may be premature because of an enormous number of young people coming into the reproduction age group, particularly in the poorer countries.

The Industrial Revolution and its effects had reached around the earth. Yet despite the overall improvements in man's condition, the benefits from the technological advances and mighty productivity of the industrial era were very unevenly distributed. Near the end of the era the world was divided into essentially two worlds: the rich, industrial world that lay to the north, and the poor, predominantly agricultural world to the south. Due to the sharply uneven distribution of the benefits of man's industrial interventions, people in the rich world (roughly one-third) were predominantly urban, industrial, literate, affluent, consumption oriented, overfed, and overweight. Life expectancy at birth was near seventy years, economic opportunities plentiful, and social mobility relatively high. Populations in the poor world (the other two-thirds) were largely rural, illiterate, hungry, and malnourished, trapped in poverty, and survival oriented. Infant mortality was still high, economic opportunities scarce, and social mobility limited. This historical divergence and widening gap between entire societies that were affluent and others that were poor was something new. Before the industrial era, most societies resembled each other, with a mass of poor peasants, living at subsistence levels, and a small, rich, minority. Little difference existed between living standards of peasants anywhere across the earth: they were all materially poor, malnourished, unable to read or write, subject to chronic and debilitating disease, and expected to live not much more than thirty years. When productive capacity and living standards began to rise in Western Europe, a small economic gap opened, first between England and the rest of the world, then between industrializing countries and the rest. By 1850 the difference in income between industrial societies and the others was around two to one. In 1950 it reached about ten to one; by 1960 nearly fifteen to one; and in 1970 the gap was still widening and was predicted to reach thirty to one by the end of the century. Both rich and poor countries were growing economically at roughly the same overall rates in the last decade of the era, but population grew twice as fast in the poor countries. As a result of this and lower starting economic base, poor countries raised their per capita incomes only $10 in the 1960s, compared with $300 in rich countries. In the 1960s, the gap between rich and poor countries widened absolutely and relatively.

Near the end of the industrial era, one-quarter of the population was estimated to be living in countries with per capita incomes averaging at least $1,000 per year; more than half lived in countries where they averaged less than $100, and the rest in between. By 1970, per capita income in the United States was $4,100; in India it was $90. The annual increase of $50 billion in the goods and services produced in the United States was equal to all the goods and services produced annually in India or Africa. Reasons for the emergence of a gap between rich and poor societies during the industrial era are not well understood, although attempts are being made to explain it in terms of religion, natural resources, climate, childrearing, the structure of colonialism and a combination of these (see Berelson, 1974; Cippola, 1964; Ehrlich et al., 1976; Frejka, 1973; Howe, 1974). Whatever the causal factors, once the gap was underway after a group of industrial countries had diverged significantly from the rest of the world in their capacity to intervene in the environment and enlarge the productivity of the earth to meet human needs, it tended to perpetuate itself. At first, industrial countries used their new technological and organizational strength to extend their colonial empires throughout Asia, Africa, and the New World. Even after the colonial empires were dismantled in the twentieth century, the industrial countries used a wide range of economic policies to maintain favorable terms of trade. Consistently, policies affecting international trade discriminated against poor countries' export products. At the end of the era, the tariff structure in force charged twice as much duty on goods the rich countries imported from poor countries as from each other. This eliminated the comparative advantage of lower labor costs, discouraged industrial growth and reinforced the traditional role of poorer countries as raw-material exporters. Rapid population growth and a self-reinforcing cycle of poverty also acted to perpetuate and widen the gap.

Throughout history, population growth has created most of the increase in demand for goods. During the industrial era, rising affluence became a major force raising demands. Since midcentury each has generated about half of the overall worldwide growth in demand for goods and services. This is deduced from the fact that world output of goods and services increased roughly by 4 percent yearly between 1950 and 1970, while world population growth averaged 2 percent annually. Nearly equal at the global level, the relative force of population growth and rising affluence varies among countries and among commodities. Within the poor countries, most of the increase in consumption was due to population growth, while within rich countries, rising per capita affluence accounted for most of the increase. The amount of energy consumed per capita can be used as a rough measure of the rising human consumption levels, as well as a proxy for the growth of technology and environmental intervention during the industrial era. Energy consumption in the past has been closely associated with life-styles and the level of human living conditions. As incomes rose, the energy required for daily living climbed sharply. Earliest preagricultural man consumed approximately 1,500 calories or 100 thermal watts per person, consisting entirely of food and approximating the minimum biological requirements. Fire for hunting, heating, and cooking brought the energy intake to around 500 thermal watts. With the harnessing of draft animals for tillage and transport, winds to move boats, and water to run food and textile mills, energy consumption increased further. The large-scale use of coal in the industrial era allowed a more rapid rise; then in the twentieth century, petroleum, hydroelectric power, the atom, and tidal and geothermal powers brought extraordinary increases in the amount of energy available. The human energy curve began to climb very sharply, reaching an average of almost ten thousand thermal watts per person in the United States; 100 times that of preagricultural ancestors.

Modern, high-income man is an enormous energy consumer, using a vast variety of energy for mobility, for producing, preparing, cleaning, and cooking food; for lighting and heating; for communication; and for information processing. Energy-intensive technology has not only brought high-income man the affluent life; it has also made him highly vulnerable to any threat to his energy supply.

As of 1970, the scope of economic activity was expanding everywhere, fueled by both population growth and the universal desire for greater affluence. Whether incomes were $90 per year in India, Bolivia, or Ethiopia, or $10,000 per year in some communities in the United States, people appeared to be interested in consuming. In the post-World War II period, there was a virtual explosion in human economic activity. The annual production of goods and services worldwide in 1950, totaled roughly a trillion dollars. By the early 1970s, the world's economic output had reached $3 trillion. During the 1960s, the yearly per capita income climbed when the *economic* growth rate worldwide neared 5 percent annually with *population* growth at 2 percent. Advancing technology and gains in productivity brought a wealth of goods and services to populations in the rich countries. For example, a range of fresh and frozen foods became available year around through advances in food preservation, transport, and marketing. Reduced transportation costs put air and international travel within the range of millions who previously could not afford it. Air conditioning, television, and rising overall beef consumption became commonplace as incomes rose in western countries and Japan. Americans had not just one car but two or three in a family, bringing unprecedented individual mobility. New synthetic fabrics, household appliances, and prepared foods lifted old forms of drudgery from housework. Contraception technologies presumably decreased the fear and increased the enjoyment of sex. A new vaccine eliminated, at least for the time being, *poliomyelitis*. Extending the horizons of his knowledge, exploration, and excitement, man rocketed to the moon and outer space. In the poorer countries, life expectancy increased steadily as expanded food supplies and improved nutrition for many were created by the green revolution. Steel plows, transistor radios, and electric lights were found in thousands of villages in Africa, Asia, and Latin America. Earlier, a 5 percent economic growth rate would have brought widespread improvements in the quality of life and conditions of human existence. Well-being has been closely associated with the trends in the production of goods and services, although not synonymous with it. Even if most of the population would have agreed that the quality of life in material terms had a net improvement in the 1960s, it was certainly no longer unquestioned. In 1950, there were few signs of stress on the natural and social systems. By the early 1970s, there were many more signs of stress on the natural system and much more competition for scarce resources both within and among nations.

In the effort to meet his needs, man is forced to intervene more and more in the natural system, altering it either directly or indirectly, as population and consumption levels rise. Take just food for example. In the world as a whole, population growth is probably responsible for 60 to 80 percent of the 2.5 to 3 percent yearly increase in the demand for food. In most of the poor countries increase in demand for food is attributable to population growth. However, rising incomes are generating even more growth in demand in Japan and in many western European countries. The effect of rising incomes on food requirements can perhaps best be indicated by observing the amount of grain required by high-, middle- and low-income populations, at current dietary levels. Grain is a good indicator of food requirements since it accounts for more than half of the direct food energy intake and is important when consumed indirectly in the form of livestock. People living in the poor countries have available about 400 pounds of grain per person yearly or about one pound daily. Nearly all of this must be consumed directly simply to meet minimal body energy needs. Very little is left to be consumed indirectly through grain-fed animals.

Moving up the scale, middle-income Europeans consume about 1,000 pounds of grain per person per year and have a diet much richer in animal products. As incomes rise, the amount of grain per person that is directly consumed declines. The amount of grain used per person climbs as more is fed to livestock indirectly. The average North American requires 2,000 pounds of grain each year. Only about 200 pounds of this is eaten directly as breakfast cereals, breads and cakes. It is mostly consumed indirectly in the form of meat, milk, and eggs. This high consumption of livestock products places enormous claims on agricultural resources since the luxury of tastier and more nutritious livestock proteins are based on the highly inefficient conversion of grain into animal products. If income levels in countries of middle or low affluence rise, their demand for diets richer in animal products will also rise. The medium United Nations' population projection for the year 2000 is 6.5 billion (Berelson, 1974; Frejka, 1973; Hardin, 1974). If this were to materialize, together with hoped for improvement in diets, the world's food requirements could enlarge by two and a half or three times the present level in this final quarter of the twentieth century. Stated another way, the increase in the earth's food-producing capacity over the next quarter-century would have to *match and go beyond* that developed from the time agriculture was invented until the present. This is not a welcome prospect in ecological terms, nor in terms of the quality of life (M.I.T., 1970). For the net result of population growth and rising incomes is mounting agricultural pressure on the ecosystem. The key question then that must be asked and answered is: Will earth's ecosystem, already showing signs of stress and strain, hold up under such growing pressure?

The crowning achievement of the industrial era was the universal adoption of the goals of sustained economic growth and ever-rising material standards of living. But a finite biosphere (Flanagan, 1970) cannot accommodate an infinite, expanding world economy, fueled both by increases in population and by human desires for continually rising material affluence. Man's interventions and their consequences were simple and localized at an earlier time but now have grown and become more intricate, widespread, and worrisome. The complex of natural cycles and systems, and the interdependent species of plant and animal life they support, constitutes a very fragile structure. This structure can be easily upset by human intervention on the scale and intensity now occurring with modern technologies and levels of economic activity. Man, one species among millions, has reached the point where deliberate and weighty thought about his interaction with the environment is required.

# 4 A New Era of Accommodation

Now being recognized more widely is the fact that the human species is moving through a discontinuity with the past, and entering yet a new era in its occupancy of the earth, an era that will be defined by the need to accommodate human numbers and ways to what is a finite planet. This era was ushered in not by a major new technology, such as the invention of agriculture, or by a host of new technologies like those associated with the Industrial Revolution, but by approaching, perhaps already exceeding, some limits of the earth's ecosystem. Resource scarcities and mounting ecological stresses signal this new era.

The approach to the earth's limits came sooner than expected. Even *The Limits to Growth* placed it a century in the future (see Meadows et al., 1972). Around 500 years ago, man discovered with certainty that the planet was globular and finite. Yet right through most of the industrial era the earth might as well have been infinite, for its bounty of resources far exceeded man's needs, even his vision of need. Its resiliency in the face of human activity was apparently sufficient. In the world as a whole, vast areas of fertile land awaited the plow. Fresh water was abundant, petroleum reserves seemed endless, and the regeneration of the earth's forests exceeded man's harvest. The oceans appeared to hold more fish than could ever be caught. Only a few localized ecological stresses were visible. Certainly the earth's climatic system seemed infinitely beyond man's touch, as did the protective ozone shield between earth and sun.

But in the early 1970s, the assumption of boundless abundance fell. World markets for energy, food, forest products and critical minerals suddenly changed to terms favoring sellers. Access to needed supplies replaced preoccupation with access to buyers that had previously characterized the major producing nations.

## RESOURCE CONSTRAINTS

While scarcities of various resources have come and gone for centuries, the problem of resource scarcity is not temporary. Technological advance may alleviate an emerging resource constraint, but the overall trend is toward chronic scarcity of many resources on which humans have grown to depend upon. While "priced" by the market, these resources have been thought to be essentially unlimited. The removal of a generalized condition of resource scarcity through technological advance does not appear to be likely, as the scale of global economic activity enlarges and pressures on the earth's finite resources become more competitive and intensify. Not all scarcities are the immediate result of present physical shortages in the earth's ecosystem or the biosphere. Often, more immediate causes are by ecological, political, technological, or economic constraints. Beneath these, however, are fundamentally changing supply and demand conditions, the effect of which will first be seen in sharply rising prices. Nor are these causes independent of one another. Fuel scarcity, for example, exacerbates water, fertilizer, and thus food scarcity. Water and waste absorption scarcities exacerbate fuel scarcity. Evidence of both the changing fundamental situation and the interdependence of resource problems is mounting, as a number of specific worldwide resource "crises" are surfacing.

**Energy, food, and water** In the early 1970s, a worldwide "energy crisis" occupied the headlines, which proclaimed shortages and quadrupling prices of energy. By the mid-1970s, it appeared clear that fossil fuels such as coal, petroleum, natural gas, and lignite were becoming scarce, and the prospect was for increasing scarcity with rising costs to continue throughout the remainder of the century. Man's strong reliance on fossil fuels for his energy supply, though two centuries old, can be but a short episode. These energy sources are not renewable over any time span meaningful to man. They are formed by the influence of solar radiation on carbon dioxide and water in living organisms, and are in essence, stored sunlight, fuel wealth accumulated in the earth over millions of years. Man has been living through the dissipation of this wealth at a rate which has been described as a weekend bonfire (see Howe, 1974; Steinhart and Steinhart, 1974; Ward and Dubos, 1972).

Energy is available in various forms ranging from fossil fuels, wood, sunlight, wind, controlled nuclear fission and fusion reactors, to geothermal, tidal, and ocean heat resources. Energy scarcities man faces in the 1970s do not reflect a long-run shortage of earthly energy as such. But they do reflect a scarcity of cheap, convenient, mobile, and formerly abundant forms of energy. The oil shortage was triggered by the 1973 Mideast Arab oil producers' decision to reduce crude oil production, and by the shortage of western refining capacity. The prospect was for continuing government limitations on future extraction rates in several oil-producing (Organization of Petroleum Exporting Countries) OPEC states. Producing energy fuels from more remote petroleum, solar, nuclear, or geothermal sources is a long and costly process. At this point, most authorities agree that a return to an abundant and cheap form of energy, if ever, awaits a breakthrough in nuclear fusion power. But the nuclear possibility believed by many to be the ultimate solution is still fraught with technological uncertainties and dangers to human well-being. This could require another fifteen to thirty years of research and development, although a better understanding of thermonuclear activity on the sun's surface could shorten this period.

If the cost of energy continues to rise, the availability of energy-intensive goods and services, including food, will be affected. In the future, man can be expected to either rely more on nuclear sources, on his own energies, or turn to renewable energy such as the sun, tides, earth heat, tropical waters and atmospheric electricity—sources now considered esoteric. He may turn to an entirely new, as yet unknown, source.

Food shortages and soaring food prices emerged in the first half of the 1970s, due partly to bad, sometimes catastrophic weather occurring in the period 1972 through 1974 in parts of Asia, Africa, the Soviet Union, and North America. But disturbing secular trends in the world food economy underlay the bad luck of the 1972-1974 harvests. World population growth and rising affluence were expanding demand for food at an unprecedented rate, outstripping food production. Demand for cereals, a good indicator of world food demand, expanded to around 30 million tons a year compared to 12 million in 1950. The result was a rapid decline of the world's two principal food reserves, and buffers against the weather and marketplace: idled cropland in the United States, and carry-over grain stocks held in exporting countries. Rice and wheat prices tripled and soybean prices doubled within a two-year period as severe competition developed among nations for available supplies. Throughout the world, for many, starvation resulted, as the nutritional well-being of low-income people was reported to be severely affected, particularly in that sizable segment of mankind that spend 80 percent of their income on food. Moreover, the world fish catch, which climbed steadily and rapidly since 1950, has declined since 1970. Meanwhile, the four major resource inputs in food production—energy, water, arable land, and fertilizer—are all in tight supply. This accentuates food scarcity and clouds future food prospects. These four productive elements will become even more crucial as world demand for food climbs, making the production of more food more costly. The world over, farmers are faced with rising costs for their essential resources. Complicating the picture is the concern of some climatologists that prevailing climate and weather conditions may be subject now to instabilities or change. This is highly perturbing because of the extreme and growing dependence of the whole world's welfare on the food resources and climate of one geoclimatic region: the North American breadbasket. This extreme dependence is historically unmatched. An adverse turn in weather in North America would have unprecedented and far-reaching effects, particularly in the absence of adequate world food reserves.

Fresh water, likely to be the principal constraint on future food production, has already emerged as a severe constraint on the expansion of both agricultural and industrial activities around the world. Vast areas of fertile but dry land now lie uncultivated. Shortage of water has restrained Soviet efforts to bring marginal land under the plow and has limited the spread of new high-yielding cereal varieties. The demand for fresh water is expected to almost triple by the end of the century. With most easily tapped rivers of the world already developed for irrigation, significant expansion of fresh water supplies will involve more unconventional intervention into the hydrologic system—such as rainmaking and desalting of seawater. Large-scale desalination awaits a much more economic source of power than any now existing. While the technology for and the pressures to use climate modification are advancing, its effects on the larger climate system and on neighboring nations are not known. As population pressures and incomes have increased in the last few decades, competition and conflict over the earth's fresh water supplies have become intense.

**Fertilizer and arable land**  The prospect in the 1970s will be for chronically tight supplies and higher prices of fertilizer. One reason for this is the energy crisis. Roughly one-half of all fertilizer used is nitrogen based, and natural gas or *naphtha* is a raw material used in the production of nitrogen fertilizer. Another reason for the shortage is the lag in production facility construction, which requires an enormous capital input. High energy prices are likely to keep fertilizer prices from falling to levels of previous decades, even when production capacity increases to meet demand. While the industrial nations have been the suppliers of chemical fertilizers in the past, the developing nations can be expected to take on this role in the future.

Population growth and rising incomes continue to increase residential, recreational, and industrial uses of land, reducing the amount of land available for food production. There is little unused but readily arable land which may still be converted to agriculture, and the 50 million acre reserve in the United States is no longer idle. Possibilities do exist, however, for expanding the world's cultivated area, but only at substantial costs. Sub-Saharan Africa and the interior of

Brazil and other Latin American countries are the only major regions where sizable portions of well-watered, potentially arable land exists. Yet the cost of producing food there may be prohibitively expensive. The tropical forest ecosystems are fragile and any expansion in these areas awaits further improvements in the ability to manage tropical soils. Once the lush, protective natural vegetation is removed, mineral nutrients can be easily leached from unprotected soil by heavy rainfall. The remaining red or yellow soil, rich in iron oxide and alumina, is relatively infertile and easily converted to a bricklike rock known as *laterite* when exposed to sun and air. Laterization, thought to have undermined the great irrigation-supported Kmer civilization in Cambodia centuries ago, in less than five years turned farm fields into rock at Iata, Brazil's experimental agricultural colony. The opening of large regions in sub-Sahara Africa to grazing and cultivation awaits eradication of the fly-borne cattle-killer disease, *trypanosomiasis*, affecting one-third of the continent, and the debilitating human disease, *onchocerciasis* or river blindness, affecting up to one million Africans.

It is true that higher and drier land, even the slopes of the Himalayas, could be cultivated if the costs were willing to be paid. Farming coastal dry lands awaits a reduction in the cost of desalinization or the technological capacity to move rainfall inland from the oceans to the land. However, the fact that most of the increases in world food output in the twentieth century has come from increasing yields on already cultivated land indicates the greater costs of bringing more marginal land under the plow.

**Minerals** By 1970, it was clear that countries which industrialized first were depleting their indigenous supplies of raw materials and that mining more remote and lower grade supplies was becoming very expensive. Meanwhile, world demand for every important mineral resource is increasing at an extraordinary rate. According to a Stanford Research Institute Report (Haddeland, 1969), the time it takes for the consumption of many important industrial minerals to double is surprisingly short: aluminum, nine years; iron, ten to fifteen years; copper, twelve to fifteen years; zinc, seventeen years; and lead, twenty years. Most countries already depend upon imports for most, and in some cases all, of their fertilizers. Thus, growing international competition, rising prices, and uncertainty over the future of many key mineral resources can be anticipated. The United States now dominates world mineral consumption, using one-fifth to one-half of most minerals. In per capita terms, industrial societies consume twenty times as much mineral ore as poor countries. As consumption levels in the poorer countries begin to rise, the worldwide adequacy of supplies will become a more pressing concern. Meanwhile, availability depends on the willingness of raw material producer countries to give access to supplies needed elsewhere. The earth's capacity to supply minerals such as bauxite and aluminum, on which industrial man depends, is very large. But by the end of the century, projected needs of now essential metals such as lead, tin, copper, and zinc will exceed projected reserves. Recycling techniques will help and advancing technology will allow some substitution, but tighter mineral obstructions to world production is probably in the future.

**Forest products and waste absorption capacity** One of the quieter dramas unfolding is the progressive deforestation of the earth. Due to agricultural expansion and firewood consumption in the developing countries, and industrial development worldwide, the consumption of forest products for fuel, lumber, and newsprint is exceeding the regenerative capacity of the world's forests. The shrinking of forests around settlements in Asia, Africa, and Latin America is causing a second energy crisis. Increasing demand and a dwindling resource capacity is accelerating prices and shortages on a worldwide basis. The trend is toward a growing scarcity of firewood in the developing world and global scarcity of newsprint and lumber, even with the use of fast-growing tree varieties. Partly because of the disturbing ecological threats to humans resulting from the earth's deforestation, this crisis will gain much more worldwide attention (Eckholm, 1976).

Since man's beginning, natural systems and cycles of air, water, and soil have been depended upon to dispose of wastes safely. But in the 1970s, this critical "resource" is in short supply. As the damaging consequences become more apparent and human tolerance of the overloading of earth's waste absorption systems decreases, the "resource" will become even more constrained.

## ECOLOGICAL STRESSES

Few ecological stresses or adverse consequences of rising activity and environmental intervention and impact were evident twenty-five years ago. Human numbers and economic output were much less, but since then, world population has jumped from 2.5 billion to 4 billion and world economic output tripled. Thus, ecological stresses have become more visible and frequent. Among the more portentous stresses are: climate modification, new threats to human health, loss and endangerment of species, eutrophication of fresh water bodies, and massive soil erosion and deterioration.

**Climate modification** Climate modification is perhaps the most dramatic of these ecological stresses. It is likely to become the foremost environmental concern in the decades ahead. There is no doubt that man's activities have altered climate locally and regionally over the millennia, but particularly in recent years (National Academy of Sciences, 1975). Climatologists now agree that human activities are of a scale and type that can inadvertently affect the earth's climate as a whole—although exactly how much is not yet clear. This is particularly disturbing in light of growing understanding of the earth's climatological history and system. Apparently, the earth has undergone far more frequent climate fluctuations and more numerous ice ages than heretofore thought. Relatively small changes in temperature and closely related conditions can induce long-term changes affecting the entire system. There are triggering points in the system such as the Arctic and the Antarctic, where changes in conditions ramify throughout the whole system. The mainly beneficent temperature and condition that have prevailed across much of the earth in the late nineteenth and twentieth centuries are historically atypical. According to climatological data, the earth's average temperature rose about 0.4° or 0.5° centigrade or one degree fahrenheit between 1880 and 1940. It has declined one-half a degree fahrenheit since then. Some scientists feel that an artificial rise in atmospheric particulate

matter may be reducing the amount of solar energy reaching the earth.
There are numerous human activities that could alter global climate: burning of fossil fuels, creating agricultural dust bowls, deforestating large areas, constructing macroengineering projects, developing the Antarctic, and directly modifying the weather. But climatic change may also result from long-term natural cycles, volcanic eruptions, or some other natural factor, or combination of factors. Because of its widespread and profound significance, climate modification has to be virtually on the top of the agenda of understandings to be developed in this new era. (See M.I.T., 1971 and National Academy of Science, 1975.)

**New health threats** As a consequence of the accelerating economic activity and environmental alterations in both industrial and agricultural societies, entirely new threats to human health have emerged. Levels of toxic substances such as lead, mercury, cadmium, arsenic, and selenium have been raised. Wholly man-made compounds, released by the thousands over the past thirty years, have been mainly unregulated. Conditions conducive to the rapid spread of certain infectious diseases have been created. The atmosphere's narrow ozone layer that protects life from lethal ultraviolet rays has been altered. Toxic substances and other environmental threats adversely affect the heart, throat, lungs, kidneys, intestines, liver, blood, genes, central nervous system, and brains of humans.

Mercury, released from both agricultural and industrial sources, is one example of a toxic substance causing concern. It is apparently in the environment at levels higher than normal—particularly in a number of animals at the top of the food chain—a fact which surprised, mystified, and alarmed many scientists. Mercury poisoning is insidious, causing a wide range of disorders from fatigue and headaches to partial deafness and death. When it reaches certain levels in water, fish, and other foods, it can cause irreversible damage to the brain and central nervous system of man and other complex organisms. Although its danger has increased, mercury has been a localized hazard for centuries. The felt hat industry of the last century exposed workers to mercury fumes which caused neurological damage and gave rise to the phrase "mad as a hatter." Dangerous levels of mercury, mainly from industrial wastes, were discovered in Lake Michigan and in the waters of more than thirty other states and Canada. Early in 1971, quantities of tuna and swordfish were withdrawn from U.S. markets after levels were discovered higher than established tolerance levels. The governments of both Sweden and Japan have recommended reduced fish intake to avoid bodily accumulation of mercury particularly in Japan where mercury from tainted fish has affected entire villages, causing illness, birth deformity, and death. Death from mercury has also been reported in West Pakistan, Guatemala, and Iraq.

Air pollution has become a health threat across the world, reaching alarming levels in many cities. Children are kept indoors or periodically cautioned against vigorous play due to air pollution levels. Medical studies have indicated a strong relation between air pollution and respiratory diseases, particularly bronchitis, emphysema, and lung cancer (Lave and Seskin, 1970).There is now mounting evidence of the contribution of air pollution to coronary disease and stomach cancer. Environmental pollution, including air pollution, may at least partially explain why life expectancy among Americans did not increase significantly during the 1960s despite impressive advances in medical technology and a vast rise in health service expenditures.

Across the poorer tropical regions of the world there has been a substantial increase in the debilitating, infectious disease *schistosomiasis,* or bilharzia. The snails which carry the schistosomiasis-producing fluke thrive in perennial irrigation systems, where they are in close proximity to large human populations. The tiny schistosome worms penetrate the skin of humans, migrate through the bloodstream, lodge, then reproduce in the liver. Eggs are then excreted with human wastes. The Chinese call this disease "snail fever" and are waging an all-out campaign against it, but schistosomiasis might also be called the poor man's emphysema because it, too, is enviromentally induced through conditions that have been created. The incidence of schistosomiasis is rising rapidly as the world's large rivers are harnessed for irrigation. It is the world's leading infectious disease, now that malaria has been reduced, and afflicts an estimated 250 million people, or one out of sixteen people living in the world today.

There is no way to know precisely how many humans are affected by already identified new health threats. One could conservatively say, however, that at least several hundred million people are suffering from environmentally induced illness growing out of human alterations of the environment.

**Loss of species**   No one knows exactly how many species of birds, mammals, and plants are threatened by agricultural and industrial activities which destroy animal habitats and introduce toxic materials into the environment. An average of one species per year made its exit from the world during this century. As the number of human beings rose, the number of other species has dropped. The Department of Interior's list of endangered species within the United States totaled seventy-nine in early 1970; now it totals more than 100. One recent worldwide list of endangered animal species, although far from complete, includes almost 1,000 species of birds, mammals, reptiles, fish, and amphibians (Curry-Lindahl, 1972). While humans are threatened by environmental alterations, many other species have a much lower tolerance. Almost everyone knows that the peregrine falcon, the world's second fastest bird, and the bald eagle, the U.S. national emblem, are threatened with extinction through nonbiodegradable pesticides. In Asia, numerous mammals are being endangered by the explosive increase in the human population and the attendant acceleration of interaction with the environment. The Bengal tiger became the target of a world rescue effort in 1972. No more than 2,000 wild tigers live in India now in contrast to forty years ago when an estimated forty to fifty thousand prowled jungle and forest habitats. Fewer than twenty clouded leopards reportedly remain in Bangladesh's Chittagong hill tracts. The number of orangutan remaining in Indonesia has dropped below 4,000. Wild elephants in Sri Lanka, their sources of subsistence diminishing steadily as forest and jungle habitat is cleared to produce food, now number no more than 2,500, less than half the elephant population of twenty years ago.

According to *Pravda*, Russia's second largest newspaper, the question of extinction of species "is worrying us more and more every year. Why do we see almost no flocks of geese and cranes in April? Almost all the partridges are gone. Our woods, gardens and fields are becoming quieter and quieter" *(New York Times, 1970)*. The reckless use of chemical pesticides is decimating various forms of wildlife in the Soviet Union, causing many species to become zoological rarities. In 1970, the duck hunting season was reportedly canceled because of the diminishing flocks of wild ducks. The return of some ten thousand storks from wintering in North Africa has long been a national event in Denmark. That number has dropped to seventy pairs in the early 1970s. Pesticide use to protect crops in the Nile valley and in East Africa is believed responsible.

A large number of species threatened may already be doomed to extinction, either because their numbers are already too small to perpetuate the species, or because the conditions threatening their survival, such as the levels of DDT, cannot be altered in time. The sad thing is that a species that becomes extinct is lost to us, to our children, and to their children for all time to come. There is no clear way to set a value on the loss of one or many species; little is understood of the effect on the web of life through the loss of a particular or of large numbers of species, including microscopic ones.

**Eutrophication of fresh water bodies**  The greatly expanded use of chemical fertilizers, particularly since mid-century has clearly been beneficial, but it has also stressed the earth's ecosystem. Chemical runoff from farmlands into ponds and streams causes the overfertilization of fresh water bodies, a phenomenon known as *eutrophication*. Eutrophication can occur over geologic time through natural processes; however, it has been greatly accelerated by human activities. Organic nitrate and phosphate introduced into fresh water serve as rich nutrients for algae which thrive and multiply rapidly. This population explosion of algae depletes the oxygen supply in lakes, streams, and rivers, killing fish, beginning with species having higher oxygen requirements. Eutrophication is reducing the fish catch from fresh water lakes and streams and even from parts of the ocean. Decomposing of the massive algae population also produces foul odors, making water unfit for recreational uses.

Lake Erie is a classic model of advanced eutrophication, receiving nutrients from both agricultural and industrial sources. Even Lake Tahoe in the United States and Baikal in the Soviet Union, two magnificent and huge fresh water bodies, are affected by eutrophication. Lake Baikal once contained the world's purest water with more than 1,000 unique species of plant and animal life.

In recent decades, new rice strains boosted rice output in the Philippines but runoff from the fertilizer used caused eutrophication and reduced fish supplies in local lakes and ponds. No one is maintaining an inventory of fresh water bodies threatened by eutrophication, but hundreds, probably thousands of lakes, streams, and ponds are affected in North America, Europe and now in the poor countries. How much fertilizer runoff is contributing to the eutrophication problem and how much can be attributed to other causes, such as animal waste runoff from feedlots, municipal and industrial waste carrying phosphates, and nitrates from internal combustion engines, remains an open question and varies from one situation to another.

**Soil erosion and deterioration** With most of the world's readily arable land being farmed, further expansion of cultivated areas involves bringing increasingly marginal land under the plow. Usually, this land has a thin mantle of life-sustaining topsoil only inches deep, that will not endure continuous and intensive cultivation. It takes centuries, sometimes millennia, to create an inch of topsoil through natural process. In some areas of the world, destroying this layer is done in only a fraction of the time. Literally millions of acreage of cropland in Africa, Asia, Central and Andean America, and the Middle East are being abandoned each year because severe soil erosion by wind and water has rendered the fields unproductive or at least incapable of sustaining local inhabitants using existing technologies. This ecological undermining has totally destroyed the earth's food producing capacity in local areas, and an inventory of regions in danger is sorely needed.

Meanwhile, fuel needs have long exceeded the replacement capacity of local forests in many parts of the world. Particularly in the densely populated poor countries, forested areas have declined to the point where there is little forest left. One such area is the deforested India-Pakistan subcontinent where cow dung must be used for cooking and heating, thus preventing the organic nutrients from being returned to the soil. Today the number of people in the world relying on cow dung for fuel probably far exceeds those using natural gas or oil. Human population growth in the poor countries is almost always accompanied by a nearly commensurate increase in livestock population. As the numbers of animals grow, they overgraze, denude the countryside of its natural grass vegetation cover, and damage trees and shrubs. Overgrazing by animals, together with progression of deforestation by humans, is almost totally stripping the countryside in poor countries, creating conditions for rapid spread of soil erosion by both water and wind.

The soil erosion problem does not end with the loss of topsoil. Much of the eroded soil is washed by streams and rivers into irrigation canals and reservoirs. The recently constructed Magla Reservoir in West Pakistan has had its life expectancy cut from one hundred to fifty years due to silting. Much soil is also lifted into the atmosphere where it may affect the earth's climate. Moreover, both flood and drought become more severe as the natural cover that normally holds soil and retards water runoff is reduced. Eventually local and regional weather patterns are altered. History gives many examples of soil abuse. North Africa, once the fertile granary of the Roman Empire, is now mostly desert. Bare countrysides in Greece, Spain, China, South Korea, Central and South America were once covered with forests and grasslands. During the early decades of this century, the United States overgrazed and overplowed the southern Great Plains, while gradually worsening wind erosion culminated in the dust bowl era of the 1930s. Fortunately, the United States had the resources and technical know-how to reverse the process by planting rows of trees and windbreakers and by fallowing large acreages. Had the United States been unable to respond in this fashion, much of the southern Great Plains would now be abandoned instead of highly productive.

Densely populated regions such as western India, Pakistan, Java, Central America, and north China are faced with similar soil erosion problems, but cannot afford to fallow large areas because food needs are too pressing. Preserving soil requires a massive effort, involving reforestation of hundreds of millions of acres, the controlled grazing of cattle, terrain contour farming, and systematic management of watersheds. Should it be established that an increasing amount of particulate matter in the earth's atmosphere is contributing to the earth's cooling trend, the richer countries would have further reason to provide massive technical and capital assistance to the poor countries to confront together this common threat to humanity. Certainly the poor countries do not now have sufficient resources to reverse this trend.

**Malfunctioning ecosystems** Any one of the above stresses is worrisome enough in itself, but in addition, these effects are symptoms of the overload on the earth's capacities, and perhaps signals of deeper, as yet unseen, problems in the ecosystem. In the past, ecosystems have deteriorated in local areas under the impact of human food-producing activities, becoming unable to support life at former levels. Formerly productive geographic areas such as the Sahara have been abandoned. Yet the Sahara's overall decline was not perceptible to any given generation. Civilizations like the Mesopotamian were undermined largely due to human intervention in the hydrological cycle without understanding or being able to control the adverse consequences. But in the past, there were always vast new frontiers, hospitable to human settlement; today, there are none. Nor are the environmental and social effects of ecological undermining in one geographic area confined to that area. An even greater danger is that ecosystem functioning could be impaired on a global scale, if one or more of the interconnected major global systems—the oceans, the climate, or one of the element cycles of carbon, oxygen, nitrogen, for example—were interrupted.

It is possible in many cases to act remedially and reverse the processes underway, if the seriousness of ecosystem difficulty is recognized and sufficient resources and cooperative action are mounted and mobilized—although often at great cost. Lake Erie could be reclaimed, but at an estimated $50 billion. The Chinese are currently building another great wall, this time with trees, to reverse millennia of soil abuse and erosion. If overfishing has seriously damaged the anchovy fishery off Latin America's west coast or the haddock fishery in the northwest Atlantic, it may take years to recover to full productive capacity, but they could, if given the opportunity. A plan even exists for building a 1,100 mile dam across the sea from Greenland to Norway to shut off Atlantic waters from the Arctic, so that the inflow of warm water could not melt the ice floes and possibly trigger another ice age. But other alterations are not reversible, even with huge resources and large-scale cooperative action. An extinct species is lost forever. Inadvertent climate change, once underway, may not be reversible. Change in the protective ozone layer may not be reversible. Even if DDT, mercury, and other persistent toxic substances were banned and usage halted worldwide, toxic levels would still persist for many years with still unknown effects on humans, plants, animals, and natural systems. Changing the tilt of the earth's axis by shifting masses on the earth's surface through macroengineering projects would also probably be irreversible, within a meaningful amount of time.

Despite all of the study, discussion, and writing about the unfolding environmental predicament, ignorance is still the central dimension of the problem. It is not what is known, but what is not known, that is most disturbing. While in theoretical terms, people would have admitted the finiteness of the planet and its capacities and the eventual vulnerability of natural systems to adverse human impact on even a global scale, the experiential awareness of it has not come into force until the present era, when some limits are already being approached. The problems visible may not be the most threatening. Man is adding more than a thousand new chemical substances to the environment each year, but screening the effects of only a few. With instruments for identifying and measuring pollutants just becoming available, it is not certain the major pollutants have even been identified. Moreover, knowledge gaps and uncertainties abound about already identified pollutants: their history, volume, distribution, sources, routes of dispersion, reservoirs and systems in which they accumulate, and their long- and short-run effects. Global climate is probably being altered inadvertently, but exactly *how* various activities are affecting it, or whether the net effect will be to contribute to instabilities in the climate system, or to a long-term cooling or warming of the earth, or to what social and human outcome is not certain. Unfortunately the thresholds of danger and irreversible change are not known. At what point does the progressive deforestation of the earth threaten global climate? At what point does modification of the ozone layer directly endanger life or cause climatic change? How much macroengineering alteration of river systems on a continental scale is possible before the shifting of this mass of weight on the earth's surface affects its rotation? At what level is DDT threatening to no species, to certain species, to many, to all, to humanity? Is human genetic material already being affected by the new forms and levels of radiation introduced, or by changes in the earth's chemistry? The extinction of species occurred with little forewarning in the past, and very slowly. What happens to the complex web of life as genetic material or species drop out more rapidly, or as their relative abundance changes? (See Curry-Lindahl, 1972.)

Because of the newness of oceanic pollution on a vast scale, the synergistic effects of various pollutants, and the infant science of oceanography (although rapidly developing), no one knows what the pollution thresholds are of the ocean or its semiseparate seas. Yet deliberately, and accidentally, thousands of waste products are added to the ocean which is, simply, the earth's largest lake. Included are perhaps half a million different substances, many of which are highly toxic — via rivers, direct dumping, and wind-borne and rain-borne deposits. Some semiseparate parts of the ocean, like the Baltic Sea, the Mediterranean, the Inland Sea of Japan and the Gulf of Mexico are currently experiencing various forms of ecological imbalance due to mounting pollution. Some worry that the ocean will become another Lake Erie (Holdren and Ehrlich, 1971 and Ward and Dubos, 1972).

How little is known about the consequences of some interventions, is illustrated by the now classic case of DDT, used for both agricultural purposes, and for the control of insect-transmitted diseases that have plagued tropical-subtropical regions of the earth. The Swiss scientist Paul Hermann Muller won a Nobel prize in 1948 for developing DDT. Less than a generation later industrial nations were banning its use. Today DDT is found in the tissues of animals over a global range of life from penguins in Antarctica, to the children in Thailand's villages, to your tissues and mine. No one knows what the long-term consequences of this contamination are, but it is known that even low environmental concentrations of DDT severely impair the reproductive capacity of some predatory birds and fishes. The slightest amount of DDT in the water is lethal to shrimp. In a sense, the biosphere has been an experimental laboratory, with man among the guinea pigs. Until recently, there has been very little effort to determine the various limits of the earth's ability to support human numbers and activities. No one knows how much slack remains in the system. (See for examples, Brown and Finsterbusch, 1972; Frejka, 1973; and Flanagan, 1970.) Many feel that the limit to energy production will be reached over the next century, but that the supply of energy fuels will not be the crucial limiting factor. Instead it will be the ability of the biosphere to absorb the waste heat. Determining the various limits of the earth's ecosystem will be a major effort of this new era. The cost of ignorance in the relationship between man and earth is undoubtedly enormous and growing. Lack of knowledge contributes to the inability to set standards, to regulate activity, to estimate the full cost humans and their heirs are paying to satisfy their wants, to shape tradeoffs, and to make the difficult choices needed at all levels of individual and social life. How to mount the effort to know and to rapidly and globally disseminate information acquired, in the face of a world poorly organized for such an undertaking, is surely one of the major challenges of the new era.

## CHANGING ATTITUDES AND BEHAVIOR TOWARD POPULATION GROWTH

At this time in history, there is no other single factor as important to accommodating to a finite physical system as the stabilizing of human population growth. The concensus on this has become almost universal, and the issue now appears to be not whether, but *how* and *when*. Changing attitudes and behavior toward population growth and fertility are evident almost everywhere, indicating that the process of adjusting in this area is at least underway. Concern about population growth is not new. Throughout history, there have been examples of human groups that have instituted ways to limit population expansion during adverse times or in situations of limited food and other resources, using ingenious birth control techniques as well as more extreme practices, such as infanticide and altruistic suicide among the aged. But traditionally, at least with the coming of nations, population increase has been viewed as desirable, as a means to increase strength and well-being — economically, politically, and militarily. Only since 1950 has there been a small and steadily strengthening movement of people, organizations, and governments concerned with the threat of rapid and continuing population growth. But resistance to continued population growth, mounting little by little, has, in the 1970s, risen sharply and spread widely in both rich and poor countries.

Signs of resistance include a worldwide liberalization of abortion, the Zero Population Growth (ZPG) movement, and the urging by some groups of an overall reduction in population size as more optimal and desirable for improving life and ensuring future survival. Local and state governments in the United

States and elsewhere are discouraging further population growth. A lengthening list of governments have instituted national population policies, and a growing number of countries have adopted population stability as a national goal. The 1974 U.N.-sponsored World Population Conference in Bucharest did agree on a world plan of action, although not on a timetable. The reasons for adopting such a stance vary. Some countries such as Mexico have abruptly changed their positions, after decades of pronatalism and firm opposition to family planning and birth control. One factor alarming the Mexican government was the unemployment among young entrants into the labor force, despite impressive rates of economic growth. Another factor was the failure of medical services and schools to keep up with expanding population growth. Perhaps the most potent force helping to change the traditional view was Mexico's shift to becoming a *net food importer* (in the early 1970s) after having been a *net food exporter* on the basis of a remarkable expansion in food production between 1955 and 1970. This shift was primarily due to a doubling of the population in just twenty years which more than absorbed the gains. Mexico's population grows at around 3.5 percent per year, one of the fastest growing populations in the world. Now it has a government-backed family-planning program. It is officially seeking to end the ancient cult of *machismo*. To do this, the government is not only promoting revisions in laws to give women equality at work, school, and home, but is campaigning to change the social attitudes that have encouraged *machismo*, or male supremacy, for so long. Interestingly, the first Worldwide Women's Conference was held in Mexico City in June 1975.

In India, the precipitous rise in fertilizer and energy prices in 1974 brought renewed urgency to their campaign to control population gains. In the United States, it was pollution, growing population pressures on national parks and recreational areas, urban congestion, and, in some regions, lack of water that contributed to the sharply aroused awareness of the adverse consequences of continued population growth, even in a rich, changing country. In Egypt, the reason for new government attitudes and action was the discovery that food production gains expected from the vast Aswan Dam irrigation project would be absorbed by the population increase occurring during the period of its construction (Sterling, 1971). In Chile and Colombia, the medical community was alarmed at the large number of illegal abortions. The practice has been for women to enter the hospital for treatment after private abortion attempts. In Japan, the renewed concern about population growth is due to pollution and congestion. In China it was concern about food supply and eagerness to protect the remarkable achievements made in nutrition. In densely populated Bangladesh, the threat of sheer starvation made the adverse effects of population growth troubling. Despite pronatalist policies of the French government, cramped living conditions in cities and increased employment opportunities for women have contributed to the steadily declining birthrate. In the Soviet Union, shortage of housing and relatively abundant employment opportunities for women have apparently been major factors in reducing population growth. Although there is still no government-sponsored or endorsed family-planning program in Italy, a private organization, the Italian Birth Control Association, is focusing attention on the population problem. The argument is that in this resource-poor country, improving the quality of living conditions depends on limiting population growth (Brown, 1974). And so the list goes.

As the process of recognizing the seriousness of the threats to human security and well-being continues, resistance to population growth is bound to mount. During the agricultural era the human population growth rate averaged around 3 percent per century. It rose sharply in the industrial era, reached a historical high toward the end of the industrial era, and then probably peaked sometime in the late 1960s, at just over 2 percent. It has been declining since and may be down to 1.8 percent or below. There is now growing doubt that the U.N. median projection of 6.5 billion, heretofore assumed the most likely for the end of the century, will be reached. It is now even possible that human population stability could be attained through extraordinary humane and voluntary efforts in a matter of decades and at just under 6 billion. This compares with the most optimistic U.N. projection of 10 billion in just over a century. Four developed countries — Austria, the United Kingdom, West Germany, and East Germany — have already arrived at population stability with the United States, Belgium, Finland, Sweden, Hungary, Denmark, Norway, Luxembourg, Bulgaria, and Switzerland approaching it. Developing countries whose birthrates are declining include Mexico, China, Egypt, Hong Kong, and Singapore.

While it is conceivable that human numbers could be stabilized in a matter of decades, it will be especially difficult over the next decade, particularly because of the exceptionally high proportion of the population in the fertile years due to the postwar baby boom. But if crude birthrates could be brought down substantially to even twenty-five per 1,000 population, a much smaller group would enter their fertile years just after the turn of the century. This would make worldwide stability (a balance between births and deaths) a realizable goal in the first two decades of the twenty-first century. Even if it were attained in several decades it will still leave a number of countries with formidably large populations to be sustained. Making family-planning services available to every man and woman in the world as rapidly as possible would measurably reduce population growth, as an estimated 40 million abortions annually indicates. But, as agreed at the 1974 World Population Conference (Berelson, 1974), the effort must reach far beyond universalizing family planning. It must also include: (1) creating new employment opportunities and social roles for women; (2) meeting the basic minimum social needs of all humans for nutrition, health, literacy, and old age social security; and (3) altering national social and economic incentives that encourage larger families. Fortunately, traditional perceptions of the role of women appear to be changing worldwide. If this global demographic transition occurs, it will be more like a return to demographic behavior of our preagricultural evolutionary history, than a uniquely new development. The unique period was the two-era demographic expansion that may now be ending.

## MODERATING HIGH CONSUMPTION

Two ways to reduce demand and stress on the earth's life support systems and its many finite resources are to move toward human population stability as quickly and humanely as possible and to slow down or curb the growth in individual or per capita consumption of material goods.

It is significant that critical questioning of presumed links between increasing material consumption and human well-being has emerged in the 1970s. The tendency is particularly evident among the youth and the enviromentally aware, but is by no means confined to them. If this questioning continues to translate into behavior or lifestyle changes, it would be significant for future consumption trends and for man's interaction with the environment (c.f.Murdoch, 1975; Steinhart and Steinhart, 1974; Ward and Dubos, 1972; M.I.T., 1970).

Among the affluent in advanced industrial societies, a number of factors — health, environment, economics, and morals — are inspiring the questioning of increasing material consumption and human well-being. Some planners in the developing countries are searching for newer and broader concepts and strategies of human development that move away from a near-exclusive emphasis on economic growth. Certainly the question will be asked, and the link examined and better understood, for both individual and national human well-being and security may depend more on departing from the present path than in continuing on it. Relatively modest changes in consumption among the affluent could significantly reduce pressures on scarce resources and natural systems. Some changes and adjustments such as eating less food, particularly meat, or switching to smaller automobiles and relying more on foot or bicycles and public transport, are already occurring among consumers and related industries.

## TOWARD A MORE PERSPICACIOUS TECHNOLOGY

Another salient change underway is in attitudes and behavior toward technology. By the mid-1970s, the questioning, examining, and assessing of technology had become so widespread that it was difficult to recall how recent a phenomenon it really is. The passage of the U.S. National Environmental Protection Act, the defeat of the American supersonic transport jet, the creation of the Office of Technology Assessment, and the unprecedented international effort at self-regulation of scientific and technological development among geneticists and microbiologists are indicative of the new caution. The tendency to channel technology is likely to be strongly reinforced with a growing understanding and awareness of the need to accommodate to the constraints of a finite earth. There can be little question that substantial changes in technology will take place in the next quarter-century. The need in this new era is for technologies that facilitate the accommodation of man's ways and overall consumption patterns, to the constraints and requirements of a limited natural system. Technologies are needed that are more conservative in their use of resources and natural capacities, less harmful in environmental terms, more socially equitable in their distributional consequences both within and among nations. In both rich and poor countries, these new needs will become forces affecting the whole range of technologies from the internal combustion engine, to automobile design, to building design, to agricultural and industrial production technologies, to the array of food products available in the future, to whole systems, such as health, transport, and educational systems. These new forces have already come tangibly into play and can be seen, for example, in the defeat of the supersonic transport jet (SST) in the United States. In this case, the technological opportunity to construct the world's fastest commercial transport vehicle certainly existed, but the SST was eventually defeated by new considerations such as the strong concern about the SST's power, not simply to overcome natural limits as before, but to potentially alter the environment, including the ozone layer which protects the earth from the sun, in ways too adverse to be acceptable. Another concern was the expectation that substantial use of public funds would continue to be required to subsidize the development and employment of SST's, when benefits would necessarily be confined to the very affluent since it would be a luxury to fly in an SST.

This has become a classic case of new forces rising to shape and modify the direction of technology. The tendency has always been for technology to strain toward overcoming former limits. Personal, corporate, and national pride and prestige, as well as economic power, was gained or lost by the creation of new technology.

In some cases technological change is easier than in others because substitute technologies already exist and change is under way. Biological pest controls can be substituted for more damaging chemical pesticides. More efficient and less ecologically damaging communication technologies could be substituted for transport technologies in many areas of economic activity. New food technologies already exist that make possible a varied and nutritionally adequate diet further down on the food chain by substituting vegetable oils and protein for animal protein and fat. New technologies can be expected to be developed based on the substitution of renewable for nonrenewable resources — solar energy, for other energy, for example. Recycling technologies are also emerging in both agricultural and industrial production.

Only a decade ago, a near-universal and almost blind faith existed in technology. Technology gained this high human estimation largely because of the role it played in overcoming scarcity, preventing mortality, and generally improving material well-being. Agricultural technology brought a more stable food supply and fibers such as cotton and wool that permitted humans to substitute cloth for animal skin protection. Industrial era technologies brought vast improvements in human shelter and mobility, a wealth of material goods, dramatic gains in life expectancy, and increased opportunity and choice to a widening minority of a rapidly expanding population. In an increasingly affluent and technological society such as the United States, technologies that increased the supply and the processing, storing, and transporting of food all tended to increase the quality and variety of diet. Transport advances enabled humans in affluent societies to become very mobile. Advances in communications permitted an enriched life through the wider sharing of arts and culture. All this and more helped to give technology an almost sacred place as an engine of improvement. But after reaching a point when further increases in consumption are not as unquestionably valued as they once were, or when technologies result in less and less tolerable environmental and social consequences, or when resource-intensive technologies are no longer economic, then one would expect the human community to critically reexamine the presumed connection between technological advance as it has been known and human improvement.

# DISTRIBUTION — THE NEW INSISTENT ISSUE

In an era when it is becoming more difficult to expand particular resources and the global economic pie, it is to be expected that relative emphasis will shift from expanding to dividing of the pie. And particularly to the extent that the consumption of *more* by *some*, means *less* for *others*, the legitimacy of existing patterns, trends, and means of distribution is eroded.

This issue is an ancient one, but its voice has been relatively soft. Distributional issues in the past, especially international ones, could be sidestepped more easily. In the industrial era of abundant natural resources, when there appeared to be no limit to potential supply, and when the earth could absorb man's intervention and impact without threatening change, the greater the overall consumption and the better the prospects tended to be for the poor everywhere. The economic growth prospects of the developing countries were closely tied to those of the rich countries. The more the affluent consumed, the greater the chances for export expansion and economic growth of the poor. But in this era of scarcity, ecological stress, and constraint on growth, the situation has become more complex, with contradictory effects on the poor. (See Ehrlich et al., 1976; Frejka, 1973; Hardin, 1974; and Holdren and Ehrlich, 1971.) Distribution, therefore, promises to be the insistent and central issue of the future.

This is already evident in certain subsectors of the economy, such as the world fish catch, fresh water supplies, petroleum, and critical raw materials. The oceanic fish catch is no longer expanding and may even be shrinking. Intensified fishing following World War II tripled fish production by 1968, an increase in output greater than that of any other major food commodity. Suddenly in 1969, after twenty years of unfailing annual increase, production of this seemingly inexhaustible resource dropped, falling 5 percent per capita on a worldwide basis. Output rose in 1970, but has declined since then. Overfishing of the more desirable table grade species, oceanic pollution, and the cyclical ups and downs of several principal species may have contributed to this change in trend. Meanwhile, competition for the fish supply has increased as the world demand for fish continues to climb. Rich countries invested in advanced technologies which enabled their fishing fleets to move into other ocean areas as supplies in their own coastal waters became depleted. The harvests off the coasts of poorer Southern hemisphere countries attracted the fleets of industrial nations. A number of the poorer coastal fishing countries, claiming prior rights to these offshore resources and fearing their depletion, have extended their offshore limits beyond the traditional three or twelve mile range to 200 miles. In the competition of the last few years, dozens of American tuna boats have been seized off the Western coast of Latin America for refusing to recognize the legitimacy of this extension of offshore limits.

When a particular resource can no longer be easily and readily expanded, attention turns to its distribution. In the case of the world fish catch, the issue is how to divide a finite global catch among an expanding world population. As of now, technological and economic power determine distribution with the rich countries getting roughly two-thirds of the total. A number of tough questions arise which are rhetorical for the time being, but are becoming less remote. Should the catch be apportioned equally on a per capita basis? Should a formula be used, based on nutritional need, with protein deficient countries receiving first claim on the earth's marine protein supplies? Should a different allocation of scarce or finite resources be related to the existing global distribution of wealth? If so, how? As the various limits of the earth's ecosystem are approached, questions of how to divide the earth's finite capacities and wealth as well as its sustainable levels of economic activity, may come to dominate local, national, and international affairs. In the absence of rules, procedures, and institutions, countries are using various nonmarket ways to protect or increase their shares of various resources.

The example of gasoline illustrates the issue on a national level. The market has only one response to scarcity: raise the price. As it rises, a number of options affect distribution. Society can let the market alone, with the probable eventual result of preventing poor people from driving automobiles. Or society can choose to limit the size of automobiles, which would decrease fuel consumption, reduce pollution, and alleviate traffic congestion, but more importantly, it would leave a more equitable distribution of a scarce resource: petroleum. It would also reduce the freedom of the rich, leaving them less comfortable.

In the case of finite resources, the distribution question extends not only to future generations, but it also reaches out to question the distribution of scarce resources among competing uses. To turn attention to the ancient issue of distribution head-on is a discontinuity with our past, almost single-minded, preoccupation with growth. A growing worldwide concern about the dividing of the world's wealth and resources is, in a large part, a response to the recognition of limits or constraints on expanding the productivity of the earth. Formerly, the rich could sidestep the issue, arguing that the pie, or a particular resource, could always be expanded and that the benefits of growth would eventually trickle down. What was good for General Motors was good for America; what was good for America, Europe, and Japan was good for the rest of the world. But when the pie can no longer be expanded as rapidly as in the past, the issue can no longer be easily sidestepped. This moves man away from the market and the price mechanism as the main distributor of scarce resources, and into considerations of value and philosophy. The road is a much slower one, once man moves away from the marketplace to search for value and philosophical bases for setting criteria for allocation and access. Making headway is not swift, even within a nation, let alone among sovereign and competing states. The significant development is that the process is underway and on a global level (see Berelson, 1974; Brown, 1972; Brown and Eckholm, 1974; Howe, 1974; and Ward and Dubos, 1972). Access to and allocation of resources among countries (what to do about scarce resources) have been discussed at various international forums in the 1970s: food at the first World Food Conference in Rome; fish and other marine resources at the Law of the Sea Conference; raw materials at the United Nations Special Assemblies; and petroleum at the various producer and consumer conferences. Although the related issues are just beginning to emerge, new bases for sharing global resources and new social theory can be expected in the next quarter-century. The alternative to agreeing on a set of standards, rules, and procedures is less desirable and less effective in a shrinking world. But the dominant social justice issue in the new era will be how to distribute equitably the earth's resources and wealth, not the old question of how charitable the rich should be to the poor. It should be recalled that the constraints on human activity and the need to accommodate to a finite physical system come in the wake of a two-century old revolution and movement in human rights. Requests from the poor and minorities across the world for greater sharing of wealth and opportunity have become demands.

# 5 Lifeboat Ethics?

Just at the moment when the human species is faced with the revolutionary need to adjust its numbers and ways to the limited natural system in which it lives, it is also rapidly discovering that the world is becoming increasingly interdependent. Certainly global economic, political, and ecological circumstances in the 1970s have been troubling. Whenever situations become difficult internationally, nations have tended to turn inward as they did in the 1930s, seeking national solutions for problems for which there were no purely national solutions, or turning away from global problems which could not be avoided. By the mid-1970s in the midst of the deeply troubling world food, energy, and other resource problems and mounting ecological stresses, some extreme proposals were being put forth. The most extreme of these proposals emphasized lifeboat ethics (see Hardin, 1974; Holdren and Ehrlich, 1971; and M.I.T., 1970).

This may be the polar opposite of the spaceship ethic espoused earlier by Kenneth Boulding and Adlai Stevenson. The essential idea in lifeboat ethics is that people living in a rich country (like the United States) are on a lifeboat which already holds as many as it can carry. If many more get on board, it will sink along with everyone else. The time has come to pull up the ladder and save ourselves. In a 1974 article by Garrett Hardin this line of argument and ethic was developed. A variation of the proposal is the *triage* concept based on the French military battle casualty formula. *Triage* (from the French *trier* meaning "to separate") classifies battle casualties into three groups: (1) the walking wounded — those who will make it by themselves; (2) those for whom there is no chance or possibility of survival; and (3) those who, with some attention and help, can make it. Paddock and Paddock (1967) put forward a version of the *triage* with respect to American food aid policy. The rich countries, they suggest, should make these distinctions in their relations with poor countries, select those worth helping, and abandon the others.

One major fallacy of the lifeboat ethic is that it underplays current and growing levels of interdependence, including the growing dependence of rich nations on poor nations for resources and for cooperation on a lengthening list of increasingly complex global problems in order to preserve or improve the quality of life of their populations. Whatever interdependence has evolved, particularly over the last quarter-century, is modest compared to what it will become in the next quarter-century, barring worldwide social disorganization and material decline. India, the classical food-dependent, poor nation, imports only 5 to 8 percent of its food, whereas a rich nation like Japan depends on imports for more than 90 percent of its petroleum. Even the traditionally independent United States, once possessing a virtually self-sufficient continental storehouse of energy fuels and raw materials, is rapidly being transformed to a highly dependent nation. Recently, the United States imported only a small fraction of its petroleum needs. But by 1975 — even with Project Independence — it was importing 40 percent. By 1985, with production from Alaskan oil fields, the United States is predicted to be dependent upon petroleum imports for well over half its needs. The United States was dependent on imports for more than half its supply of six of the thirteen basic minerals required by a modern industrial economy. By 1985, it is predicted to be primarily dependent on imports for supplies of nine of the thirteen minerals, including three major ones: bauxite, iron ore, and tin. By the end of the century, the United States is projected to be *importing* the major share of its petroleum, and twelve of the thirteen basic raw materials, depending, of course, on their availability and on the continued U. S. access to foreign markets for its exports on a scale sufficient to finance its required imports.

The list is long of ways in which decisions and actions taken by one nation affect the welfare of people elsewhere. Only when one attempts to inventory examples of interdependence or considers the various forms of interdependence that have emerged among the world's nations and peoples does one get some inkling of the extent of interdependence. Today, decisions taken in one country may affect more people outside that nation than within.

In part, this growing interdependence derives from the beginning of the press against the earth's capacities. The oceanic fish catch is again an example. As long as the sea held more fish than ever dreamed of being used, each country was of little concern to the other. But as the world moves into a situation in which the marine catch exceeds the capacity to replenish, then nations become interdependent, because there is no other way to preserve this important global protein resource. As economies modernize (as a result of the historically recent economic processes), nations become dependent on an extremely long list of raw materials. A subsistence economy needs land and water, and by definition is independent from the rest of the world. But very few countries, or even continents, have all the resources they need for a modern economy and are instead dependent on a flow of resources from outside. The depletion of reserves in the industrial countries makes them increasingly dependent on the imports from poor Asian, African, and Latin American countries. The relationship between rich and poor nations is becoming more genuinely interdependent in this new era, and the changed relationship to the environment brought on by economic expansion underlies that change. Interdependence has most commonly been thought of as economic interdependence. This is not surprising, given the rapid expansion of international trade in the latter industrial era as restrictions have been removed and countries permitted to further specialize in those products and commodities in which they have the strongest competitive advantage. Employment and economic growth at the national level depends upon expanding international trade. No longer are nations able to manage inflation alone. What is new also is that production itself is being internationalized through multinational corporations such as IBM in Latin America and Ford Motor Company in Asia.

Technological interdependence among nations is also a consequence of growth and modernization around the world. As technology becomes more sophisticated, no single country can remain in the forefront and conduct research in all areas. While the United States is still the dominant developer of new technology, other countries have been specializing in research and development. The Russians have specialized in extracting and mining technologies; the United States in computer technology; the Japanese in superships. American firms are buying extracting and mining technologies from the Russian government through licensing arrangements. The Russians import American computers and motors, thereby gaining technology. Countries, as a result, become dependent on each other for new scientific knowledge. Increasingly, man looks beyond national borders for technologies to solve problems or raise living levels. Technologies cross borders through private investment, the purchase of patents and licenses, through imported products, or through consultants and technical assistants.

Serious social problems have emerged in recent years in both rich and poor nations that cannot be solved by countries acting alone, and therefore the interdependence of nations is increased and the need for cooperative approaches mounts. Such social problems include drug addiction, the flow of narcotics across borders, unemployment, aerial hijacking, and terrorism. Moreover, the power of modern telecommunications is making it increasingly difficult for people in one nation to isolate themselves psychologically from what happens in the rest of the world. Adopting a lifeboat ethic, given the growing interdependence among nations and the transformation of the world from a collection of relatively independent isolated nation states, to one of complex interdependence, is probably not possible. Even if it were possible, a lifeboat ethic is not necessary, at least not now, for the following reasons:

1. *It is too soon to assess the capacity for cooperation among the world's nations.* If one takes an overall view, then one can see that global cooperation has barely been attempted by man. Even if one takes into account the abortive experience with the League of Nations and the emergence of the United Nations' family of organizations (and some other global institutions) in the past decades, the arts and efforts at cooperation are still in their infancy. Commitment to and financial support of cooperative modes of human association and activity at the global level have been meager. Certainly, cooperation among the world's nations has never before been tried in a context where the common need and demand for it, and the benefit to be derived from it, are as great as they are today in the face of a growing list of common global threats to future human well-being. Some global institutions have already served humankind well, including the International Monetary Fund, the International Bank for Reconstruction and Development (or World Bank), the World Health Organization, the World Meteorological Organization, the Food and Agriculture Organization and the more recently created, if limited, United Nations Environment Program. Most requisite institutions have not yet been created, however, for the lengthening list of global problems which can be effectively handled only at the global level; awareness of their necessity is only beginning to emerge. This may be a good thing, given the tendency toward inertia of most older, existing institutions. Certainly the common problems arising now demand new thinking, new approaches, and new forms of cooperation. Man now has the technological capacity to alter rainfall patterns; yet no agency exists to regulate such activity and

determine under what conditions a country should be permitted to alter climate patterns. No institution exists to regulate the troubled interface between uncontrolled, multinational corporations and nation states. The need to regulate the exploitation of oceanic resources is pressing, yet no effective institution has been established. One encouraging development is the global progress underway for the creation of a world food reserve.

2. *For the first time in history the world possesses the wealth and productive resources to overcome hunger and poverty, the great unfinished business of mankind.* Since hunger and poverty are no longer necessary, their continuation is a matter of human choice. This coincidence of arriving at a point of needing to accommodate human numbers and overall consumption patterns to a limited planet at a time when the world possesses such wealth and productive capacity is propitious. It did not have to occur and the fate of millions of people living in the new category of "Fourth World" countries could have been written off as hopeless. But instead, the world could actually and might well see in this new era the eradication of hunger and poverty from the planet, if it bends energies and efforts toward that end. The old view of the world growing up after World War II, consisting of East, West and Third World countries is no longer appropriate. The countries of Asia, Latin America and Africa are not an unrelieved group of Third World poor nations. It no longer makes sense to place Iran and Bangladesh, for example, in the same category when their conditions, problems, and prospects are very different.

3. *Changes are occurring on the population front.* Population growth is the major force raising the pressures and demands on the earth's resources and ecological systems. But, as indicated above, changes in attitudes toward population growth are altering and birth rates are being lowered in many rich and poor countries. If this tendency to downturn is reinforced by increased education and awareness, and even minimal expenditures in Fourth World countries to establish family planning clinics, improve food production, and in general, create a more secure and promising social environment, it is now conceivable that population growth not only could be harnessed in a humane way, but within decades, rather than a century.

4. *The high consumption levels among affluent groups in the rich industrial nations leave room for slack in the man-earth system and interaction.* The consumption levels could be reduced, and pressure relieved on the earth's capacities without necessarily lowering, and maybe improving well-being. There are some indications that rich country populations, as they are becoming increasingly aware of the continued existence of extreme poverty at a time when it is no longer necessary, are showing willingness to consume less.

Adopting the lifeboat ethic or moral framework is, to say the least, not consistent with the highest and best potentiality of the species. It would be particularly damaging morally to those people who have pride in their humanitarianism.

There will be plenty of reinforcement ahead to underscore and underpin the need for cooperative approaches to living in this new era. Admittedly, the possibility has always been that these messages will result in conflict rather than cooperation. But in a world in which conflict has enormous portentous consequences, cooperation will increasingly appeal to man's rationality.

The question still remains: will humans accommodate their numbers and ways to the finite natural system in which they live? We have occupied just a few seconds of the earth's life, and insignificant moments in cosmic time. Despite this, it is clear that what happens on or near the earth in the next few "seconds" depends, to paraphrase American astronomer Carl Sagan (1975) "on the scientific wisdom and sensitivity of mankind."

# References

**Beir, George, Anthony Churchill, Michael Cohen, and Bertrand Renaud**
1975 "The task ahead for the cities of the developing countries." World Bank Staff Working Paper Number 209. Washington, D.C. (July).
**Berelson, Bernard (ed.)**
1974 "World population: Status report; a guide for the concerned citizen. Population Council, Reports on Population/Family Planning (January).
**Brown, Lester R.**
1972 World Without Borders. New York: Random House.
1974 In the Human Interest: A Strategy to Stabilize World Population. New York: W. W. Norton.
**Brown, Lester R. and Erik P. Eckholm**
1974 By Bread Alone. New York: Praeger Publishers.
**Brown, Lester R. and Gail W. Finsterbusch**
1972 Man and His Environment: Food. New York: Harper and Row.
**Brubaker, Sterling**
1972 To Live on Earth: Man and His Environment in Perspective. Baltimore: Johns Hopkins University Press, Resources for the Future Study.
**Cippola, Carl M.**
1964 The Economic History of World Population. Baltimore: Penguin Books.
**Curry-Lindahl, Kai**
1972 Let Them Live: A Worldwide Survey of Animals Threatened with Extinction. New York: William Morrow.
**Dalrymple, Dana G.**
1974 Development and spread of high-yielding varieties of wheat and rice in the less developed nations. Foreign Agriculture Rept. No. 95. Washington, D.C.: U.S. Department of Agriculture (July).
**Davis, Kingsley**
1971 "The urbanization of the human population." In Man and the Ecosphere: Readings from Scientific American. San Francisco: W. H. Freeman and Company.
**Eckholm, Erik P.**
1976 Losing Ground: Environmental Stress and World Food Prospects. New York: W. W. Norton.
**Ehrlich, Paul R.; Anne H. Ehrlich, and John P. Holdren**
1976 World Science: Population, Resources, and Environment. San Francisco: W. H. Freeman and Company.
**Flanagan, Dennis (ed.)**
1970 The biosphere. Scientific American, September.
**Frejka, Tomas**
1973 The Future of Population Growth: Alternative Paths to Equilibrium. New York: John Wiley and Sons (Population Council book).
**Haddeland, George E.**
1969 Potash fertilizers. Rept. No. 14. Menlo Park, Calif.: Stanford Research Institute.

**Hardin, Garrett**
1974 "Lifeboat ethics: the case against helping the poor." Psychology Today 8 (September).
**Holdren, John P. and Paul R. Ehrlich (eds.)**
1971 Global Ecology. New York: Harcourt, Brace, Jovanovich, Inc.
**Howe, James W. (ed.)**
1974 The U.S. and the Developing World: Agenda for Action. New York: Praeger Publishers.
**Lave, Lester and Eugene Seskin**
1970 Air pollution and human health. Science 169 (August 21).
**McNeill, William H.**
1965 The Rise of the West: A History of the Human Community. New York: American Library.
**Meadows, Donella H., Dennis L. Meadows, Jorgen Randers, and William W. Behrens III**
1972 The Limits to Growth: A Report for the Club of Rome's Project on the Predicament of Mankind. New York: Universe Books.
**M.I.T.**
1970 Man's Impact on the Global Environment: Report of the Study of Critical Environmental Problems (SCEP), Cambridge, Mass.: M.I.T. Press.
1971 Inadvertent Climate Modification: Report of the Study of Man's Impact on Climate (SMIC), Cambridge, Mass.: M.I.T. Press.
**Murdoch, William W. (ed.)**
1975 Environment: Resources, Pollution, and Society. Stamford, Conn.: Sinauer Associates.
**National Academy of Sciences**
1975 Understanding Climatic Change. Washington, D.C.: U.S. Committee for the Global Atmospheric Research Program, National Research Council.
**New York Times**
1970 Russian reports ecology threat. April 27.
**Paddock, William and Paul Paddock**
1967 Famine 1975: America's Decision, Who Will Survive? Boston: Little, Brown.
**Sagan, Carl**
1975 A cosmic calendar. In Natural History 84 (December).
**Steinhart, Carol E. and John S. Steinhart**
1974 Energy: Sources, Use, and Role in Human Affairs. North Scituate, Mass.: Duxbury Press.
**Sterling, Claire.**
1971 Aswan dam looses a flood of problems. Life, February 12.
**Ward, Barbara and Rene Dubos**
1972 Only One Earth: The Care and Maintenance of a Small Planet. New York: W. W. Norton.

# THE BOBBS-MERRILL REPRINT SERIES

The author recommends for supplementary reading the following related materials. Please fill out this form and mail.

*Indicate the number of reprints desired.*

_____ **Davis, Kingsley** "Population Policy: Will Current Programs Succeed?" Science, 1967, pp. 730–739.  S-565/66942  40¢

_____ **Davis, Kingsley** "The World Demographic Transition." The Annals of the American Academy of Political and Social Science, 1945, pp. 1–11.  S-370/66748  40¢

_____ **Ogburn, William F.** "Inventions, Population and History." Studies in the History of Culture. Long, Percy (ed.), Menasha, Wisc.: George Banta Publishing Co. for the American Council of Learned Societies, (1942), pp. 232–245.  S-474/66854  40¢

*The Bobbs-Merrill Company, Inc.*
*Educational Publishing Division*
*4300 West 62nd Street*
*Indianapolis, Indiana 46268*

Instructors ordering for class use will receive *upon request* a complimentary desk copy of each title ordered in quantities of 10 or more. Refer to author and *complete* letter-number code when ordering reprints.

☐ Payment enclosed                    ☐ Bill me (on orders for $5 or more only)

_____Course number              _____Expected enrollment

☐ For examination                     ☐ Desk copy

Bill To _____

ADDRESS _____

CITY_____STATE_____ZIP_____

Ship To _____

ADDRESS _____

CITY_____STATE_____ZIP_____

Please send me_____copies of the sociology reprints catalog.

Please send me related reprints catalogs in _____

_____

Any reseller is free to charge whatever he wishes for our books.

*For your convenience please use complete form when placing your order.*

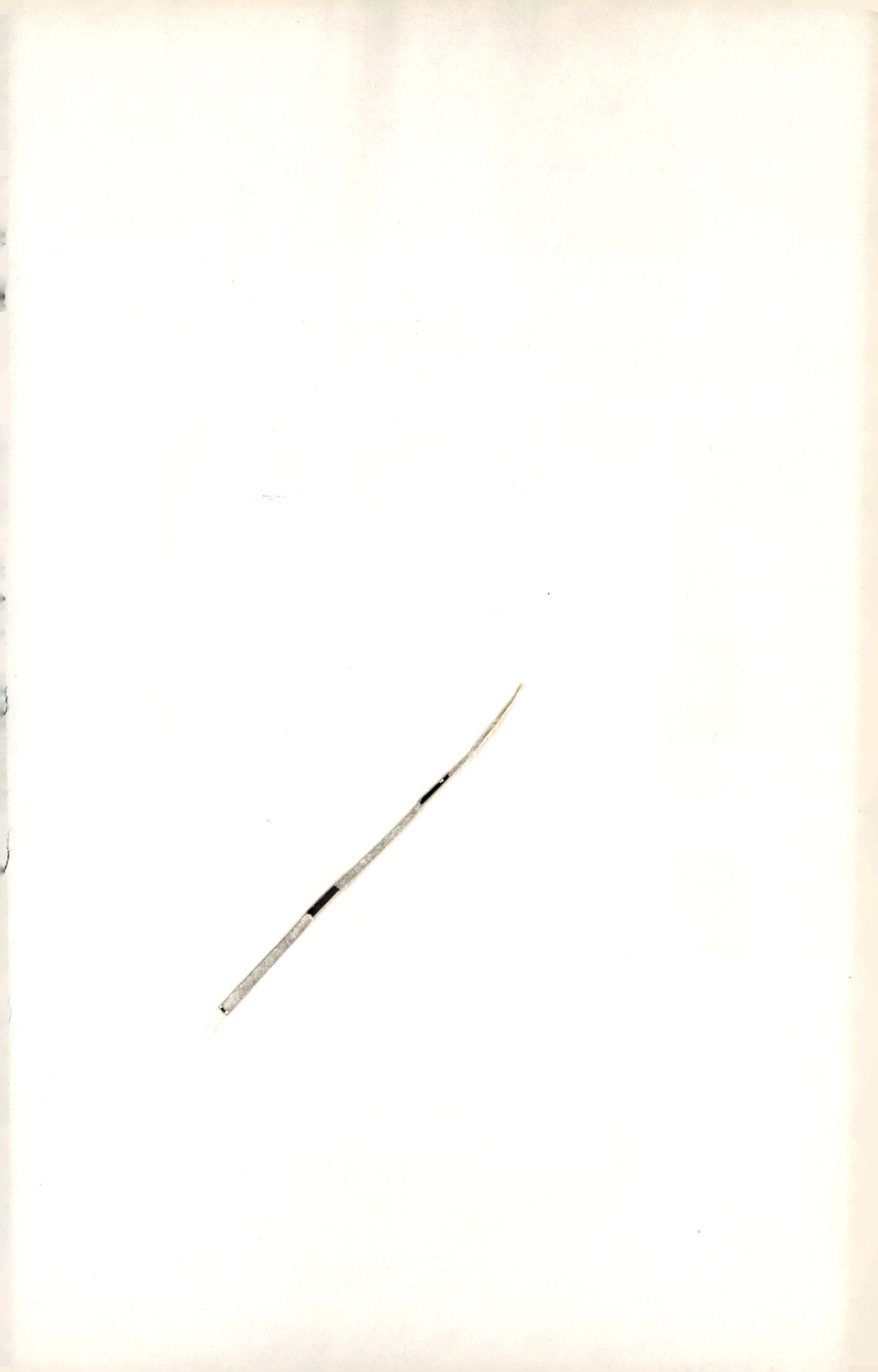